GW01044301

CALL BACK YESTERDAY

A McNaughton clansman.

CALL BACK YESTERDAY

A Memoir
Volume One

Jill Ashley Miller

STRATHMORE PUBLISHING

LONDON

2007

To my daughter Bridget,
without whom this journey would not have been made

'O! call back yesterday, bid time return'
Richard II 3.2.69

First published in Great Britain by Strathmore Publishing,
41 Kingsway Place, Sans Walk, London ECIR OLU, 2007

© Jill Ashley Miller 2007

Designed and produced by David McLean, London, in Manticore type.
Illustrations (with some exceptions) scanned and processed by David McLean

Edited by Christopher Pick

Every effort has been made to trace the owners of copyright material, both
written and photographic. If any have been missed, I can only apologise. JAM

Jill Ashley Miller has asserted her right to be identified as author of this work.

All rights reserved. No part of this book may be reproduced or utilised in any
form or by any means, electronic or mechanical, including photocopy,
recording or by any information storage or retrieval system, without
permission in writing from the author.

ISBN 978-0-9550887-3-5

Printed and bound by Portland Print, Kettering, Northants, NN16 8UN

This book has been privately printed. Further copies may be obtained from
'The Present Finder', Sherborne, Dorset, DT9 3PS
Telephone : 01935 815195 Email: info@thepresentfinder.co.uk;
www.thepresentfinder.co.uk.

Proceeds will help to support Burlingham House, Norwich, NR13 4EQ,
www.burlinghamhouse.org, the Residential Care Home where the author's
Down's Syndrome daughter is looked after.

Contents

Sir James Kitson in his study.

Preface

Soon after my husband died in September 1997, my daughter Bridget suggested that I should write my memoirs. 'We don't know anything about the lives of our grandparents, or great-grand-parents,' she said. 'It would be fun to find out.'

And so, for the past eight or nine years, this has been an absorbing and therapeutic task. It is a journey that has revealed members of my family whom I never knew existed and taken me to places far afield which I never thought to visit in my eightieth year. I have discovered long-lost cousins and renewed old friendships. It has been fun to write. Those great wordsmiths, Diana Athill (*Yesterday Morning*) and Alan Bennett (*Untold Stories*), have been my mentors.

This is only Volume One. It begins in 1685 and continues to just after 1925, when I was born. There is much more to say. I hope to be spared long enough to say it.

JILL ASHLEY MILLER
Beccles, Summer 2007

The seven Kitson sisters: Angela, Thelma, Violet, Enid, Doris (my mother), Evelyn and Sylvia. This photograph was probably taken in 1911 when, following the death of their grandfather, their father became Lord Airedale and they took the courtesy title 'the Hon.'

Acknowledgements

I have had much help with this book. First, I would like to thank my cousins, both known and formerly unknown. My third cousin, Tim Kitson, set the ball rolling with a Yorkshire visit in which he gave me much background information. My first cousins Mary Montague, Beryl Johnson and Jean Arnot joined me in Leeds where we all sifted through the vast Kitson archive. The help of my newly discovered third cousin Anthea Boylston has been invaluable. Not only did she send me many family photographs, supply information, and conduct Mary and me on a tour of Leeds; she also welcomed us to *Casa Cuseni*, the Sicilian house built by our great-uncle Robert Kitson in 1905. E.F. Clark, another cousin, has given me much information on railway history and allowed me to reproduce the de Laszlo portrait of his great-great-uncle Professor Clark, now in St John's College, Cambridge. He also provided photographs and much of the complicated Kitson family tree. My second cousin, Francis Roberts, has given me much help. Mark Landale, Stewart's grandson, lent me his letters from the front.

On the McNaughton side, I must thank another newly discovered second cousin, Donald McNaughton, who found me through a query I left on the internet. He has filled in much of the McNaughton family tree.

Most of the anecdotal evidence in the book has been taken from *James Kitson and Some Others*, the 261-page unpublished memoir which G.Talbot Griffith produced in 1970. It has been invaluable. Talbot Griffith was twice connected to the Kitsons: first through his grandmother, Clara, who married Grosvenor Talbot and was the sister of James Kitson II's wife, Emily Cliff; secondly, through his Talbot grandfather's sister Ellen, who married Frederick William, the brother of James II. Perhaps my greatest debt is to my godmother Emily for her foresight in preserving the many letters that formed the core of Talbot Griffith's book.

My thanks are also due to the staff at New Register House, Edinburgh, and the West Yorkshire Archives, Sheepscar, Leeds. Both were unfailingly helpful.

The finished shape of this book is due entirely to the design skill of David McLean, whose father, Ruari, was one of the great typographers of all time, and to Christopher Pick, whose meticulous editing has transformed a rag-bag of snippets into the polished product which you see today.

Picture Credits

p. 2 **A McNaughton Clansman** R. R. McIan *Clans of the Scottish Highlands*, Webb & Bower 1980; pp.6, 38, 56, 72, 73 Leodis – Leeds City Council www.leodis.net; p.13 **Dunnottar Castle** Colin Baxter; p.23 **Dundee to Newtyle Railway** The Oakwood Press, P.O, Box 122, Headington, Oxford; p.32 **James Kitson I**, Mayor of Leeds West Yorkshire Archives; p.43 **Robert Kitson** Daphne Phelps Bequest, Brotherton Library, Leeds University; p.48 **Professor E. C. Clark** E. F. Clark and St. John's College, Cambridge; p.51 **Mrs.William Playfair** Huntington Library, San Marino, CA USA; p.58 **Roland, 3rd Baron Airedale** The National Portrait Gallery www.npg.org.uk; pp.32, 52, 53, 60, 63, 69, 77, 96, 97, 99 West Yorkshire Archives; pp.6, 66, 67, 70 Susan Lasdun, *The Victorians at Home*, Weidenfeld & Nicolson 1981; p.71 Peter Nahum At The Leicester Galleries, www.leicestergalleries.com; p.119 Strathspey and Badenoch Herald, 11th February 1977

Every effort has been made to trace owners of copyright. If any have been missed, I can only apologise.

A croquet party at Cassilis House, 1904: from left to right: Miss Boyd; Aunt Nell (Helen Wolfe-Barry); my grandfather (the Reverend G.F.A. McNaughton); and Aunt Euphans (Euphans Strain, *née* McNaughton)

James and Ellen McNaughton, my great-grandparents

Chapter 1

The McNaughtons 1685–1897

'Time is the nurse and breeder of all good.'

The Two Gentlemen of Verona 3.1.241

One late May evening in the year 1685, a dishevelled group of 122 men and 45 women struggled up the steep and stony path to Dunnottar Castle, which lay on the rugged east coast of Scotland, just south of Aberdeen. They were known as Covenanters,[1] devout Presbyterians who refused to acknowledge the supremacy of the English King, James II, and to use the new Episcopalian prayer book. Dunnottar had been badly damaged by Cromwell's guns, but now, almost a ruin, it served as a grim fortress in which to imprison disobedient malcontents. For nearly two months, until the end of July, the prisoners were herded into an underground vault, its floor covered with midden and excrement, crowded so

Dunnottar Castle on the east coast of Scotland

13

closely together that they had to lean against each other in order to sit, with little food and water and no sanitation. The brutal English guards demanded payment for every drop of water, and when the money ran out they poured the contents of each barrel on to the mud floor, thus to compound their victims' misery. Only a few of the prisoners survived. (I have been there and it is a fearsome place even today.)

One who did was my six times paternal great-grandfather,[2] William Niven, a man whose physical courage was as strong as his moral principles. For several years he had been a trial to the English authorities on account of his refusal to acknowledge the forms of the Church of England, which he regarded as akin to popery. In 1678 he was accused of having attended a conventicle,[3] an illegal religious meeting, at Williamwood, a village 5 miles south of Glasgow.[4] He was found guilty and condemned to be transported to the plantations. With several others, he was shipped from Leith to Gravesend, but, as no ship was ready, they were allowed to go free. Nine months later he found his way home to Scotland. For several years William kept out of trouble, but in 1684 he was arrested for hearing a sermon by Mr Renwick, a noted opponent of the established church. A party of soldiers entered William's house at midnight and he was thrown into Glasgow jail, where he lay in irons for three weeks. Still refusing to take the Test,[5] he was sent with other prisoners, chained two by two, to Edinburgh jail. Prisoners were entirely dependant on their families, and William's son, also William, twice weekly walked the 60 miles between Pollokshaws and Edinburgh to deliver food and clothing for his father. During this time William senior was accused, with his Laird, Sir James Maxwell of Pollok, of affixing seditious notices to the doors of various churches and told that he would be executed at ten o'clock that night. However, the death of Charles II threw everything into confusion. William remained in prison until May 1685, but he must have lived every day in fear that the sentence would be carried out.

Early that month news reached Edinburgh that the Earl of Argyll, who had fled to Holland after a charge of high treason, had landed in Orkney with a large force of men. A staunch Protestant, he was determined that the Roman Catholic James II should not succeed his brother and that the Duke of Monmouth, Charles II's natural son, should reign instead.[6]

When news of the invasion reached Edinburgh, the authorities panicked. William and many others were hurried to Burntisland on the north shore of the Firth of Forth. There 240 wretched prisoners were thrust into two small rooms. In the foetid air and cramped quarters and with little food to sustain them, many died. On 24 May 1685 the surviving men and women were marched to Dunnottar Castle near Aberdeen, a distance of 100 miles. Here, having suffered 'intolerable hardships', 25 escaped through a window. Weak and emaciated, they crawled along a narrow ledge, 160 feet above the sea. Cruelly, they were spotted by washerwomen (probably wives of the English soldiers) on the shore below who raised the alarm. Eight managed to escape, but two fell from the cliff and were dashed to death on the rocks beneath. The remaining 15, too weak to get far, were recaptured, among them William Niven, Peter Russell and Alexander Dalgleish. They were laid on their backs on a form in the guard house, their hands bound to the form, and, with a 'fiery match' between their fingers, they were brutally tortured for three hours. William lost part of his left hand; others, less fortunate, lost their whole hands, the bones being burned to ashes. Dalgleish died after his wounds became infected.[7]

William was deported to America, sailing from Leith on 5 September 1685. No sooner had the ship rounded Land's End when a 'malignant fever' broke out, and many perished. Three or four bodies were thrown overboard each day. The Captain treated the survivors with great severity, curtailing their rations. After 15 weeks at sea living in rat-infested quarters, they landed on the shore of New Jersey. When 'the cause of their banishment was known', they were treated with great kindness by the inhabitants. Many of the prisoners settled in New England, obtaining employment according to their skills. Most died there, but a few, among whom was William Niven, eventually returned to Scotland. He was accompanied by Mr McLellan, the laird of Barmagachan, Kirkcudbright,[8] and the Reverend Mr Riddell. On their voyage home in

Dunderave castle, Loch Fyne, the McNaughton stronghold.

1689, they were captured by a French man-of-war off Nantes and thrown into Rochefort jail. Later, chained in pairs and driven on by whips, they were marched to Toulon. The elderly Mr McLellan was chained to his 11-year-old son. Eventually, an exchange of prisoners took place and William Niven was able to return home to his family, where he ended his days in the more enlightened reign of William III. Thus my ancestor proved himself to be a man of undaunted spirit, whose strength was derived, against the most brutal odds, from his unwavering faith in God.[9]

* * *

Three hundred years ago, the hills and glens of northern Perthshire swarmed with McNaughtons. They had lived and farmed for generations in the villages and hamlets near Dunkeld, in places such as Logierait, Dowally and Caputh. Some of them

16

were well-known, among them John McNaughton, a swordsman from Tullypurie, who won fame during the Jacobite uprising of 1745. Hidden in the moors and heather near his home were stragglers from Prince Charlie's army, fleeing from Culloden. Another McNaughton was Peter of 'Baile-an-Eas', whose fame as a poet and Gaelic scholar had spread much further than Strathtay, his local glen. Generous and kind-hearted, he was known as one of the region's 'Grand Old Men'.

On 27 January 1754 John McNaughton (probably a kinsman of the swordsman) was married to Jannet Sim in the kirk of Dowally. Five years later, on 26 August 1759 he was ordained an elder of that kirk.[10] Elected with him were Alexander McInroy of Balncraig, James Lord of Rierannoch and John McIntosh of Middleton of Dalkeapon. Elders were powerful people and the appointment of the next minister was in their gift. Upon his marriage, John rented the farm of Rotmell, which lies on a spur some 4 miles north of Dunkeld, just above the great road that the army of General Wade had tramped on their way to quell the Highland risings of 1745. Like most of his neighbours, he was a tenant of the 3rd Duke of Atholl, whose land covered great swathes of Perthshire.

John and Jannet were not immediately blessed with children (perhaps several did not survive the hard winters), but at last, seven years later, their son, Patrick, was baptised on 9 August 1761 at Dowally. A daughter, Jannet, followed on 8 September 1770,[11] and a second son, Donald, was baptised on 23 May 1773. The nine-year gap between the first two children suggests that there were others in between whose baptisms went unrecorded. One of these may have been my great-great-grandfather, also John.

In 1760, John entered into a joint tenancy with his neighbour, William Keir, to farm Nether Mains, part of the Rotmell estate. This partnership lasted for 11 years.[12] Other members of the Keir and McNaughton families did not get on so well. Rotmell was a tightly knit steading[13] containing seven tenants, and sometimes tempers flared. Early in the morning of Friday 28 February 1773, the 16-year-old Donald Keir and his younger brother, who had been sleeping on the hay in their widowed mother's barn,

St Colmn's, from Dalguise. 604

Rotmell Farm, Dunkeld, Perthshire.

were woken by a noise and saw their neighbour, Alexander McNaughton, climb over the wooden partition that divided their two barns and steal two baskets of oats. The boy called out 'Sanders! You have done enough,' upon which the thief jumped back into his own quarters. The brothers rose and told their mother of the theft. A few days later, young Donald saddled horses and rode into Dunkeld to sell peat, which he loaded into creels slung over the animals' backs. When her son had not returned by nightfall, the widow became anxious. Later the horses returned alone, still carrying the empty baskets, but there was no sign of the boy. Suspicion immediately fell on Alexander McNaughton, who had been seen cutting broom with a sharp hook near the Dunkeld road. A search was made, and the boy's body was found in the river Tay. It was carried to Dowelly church, where the head was found to be badly cut about by a sharp weapon. Blood was found on McNaughton's jacket. He, of course, denied murder and said he had cut his finger. The only witnesses were two small beggar boys, aged ten and nine. For several days

18

they were too frightened to speak, but eventually they said they were near Ledpetty Wood where McNaughton had been cutting broom. They heard young Donald Keir returning home with his two horses. They also heard the older man ask him if he would like to sit down and take some snuff. The boy dismounted and sat down beside McNaughton, whereupon the latter took up his hook and struck him viciously about the head. The two boys, terrified by his screams, ran home, but were too young to be called as witnesses. Although the evidence against McNaughton was circumstantial, it was supposed he had killed the boy out of revenge. He was committed to Perth gaol and was probably hanged.[14]

In a cold December in 1793, just three days before Christmas, John McNaughton's son, John, married Janet, daughter of his father's old friend William Keir, now farming at Newtown, also part of Rotmell. Their marriage, too, was blessed with progeny. Next year, on 14 November 1794, twin sons, Donald and John, were born. On 11 July 1796 a third son, Peter Patrick arrived, to be followed by four girls: Janet on 27 September 1798, Elspeth on 27 July 1800, Margaret on 8 July 1802 and Jean on 22 September 1804. There then appears to be a shortish gap, in which children may have been born who did not survive. John's tenancy continued until 1800 when Rotmell farm was taken over to form a new estate. The old farmstead was pulled down and handsome new buildings were built around a central courtyard, which exists today. This was the inspiration of Anne, the philanthropic wife of the 4th Duke of Atholl, who took a keen interest in her tenants' welfare.

Winters were hard in north-west Perthshire, and that of 1807 was no exception. Cut off from the outside world by the Grampians to the north and the fast-flowing Tay to the south, the scattered farmsteads were often isolated. Deep drifts of snow blocked the roads, and when the river was in spate its only crossing, the Caputh ferry, was unable to ply. It was at Rotmell, on a bitter winter's day when the year was barely two days old and howling winds were sweeping across the mountains, that a fourth son was born to John and Janet McNaughton. When the weather eased, and the road was cleared of snow, his father set out for Dowally, half a mile away, to register his birth. The child was named James. He, his three brothers and four sisters were joined in 1809 and 1811 by two more sisters, Helen, on 11 May 1809, and Elisabeth, on 7 August 1811. A fifth son, William, arrived on 30 May 1815. The family of eleven children was now complete.

James, my great-grandfather, flourished, tended by loving, god-fearing parents, playing with his brothers and sisters on the moors and fishing in the lochs. It was a secure and happy childhood, which doubtless accounts for his harmonious nature.

At 19 years old, intelligent, ambitious and full of curiosity, he set out for Dundee, 30 miles away. He had heard that a railway might be built linking the port with Newtyle, a small hamlet some 9 miles north. The idea of a railway link to the vale of Strathmore was first mooted by George Kinloch, a leading citizen of Dundee. At that time, the port looked seaward and the rich resources of Strathmore – particularly its flax, vital for the textile mills – were being neglected. Kinloch called a meeting, which was attended by the leading landowners, Lord Airlie and Lord Wharncliffe, and in January 1825 it was decided to go ahead. Subscribers were canvassed and (for a fee of £100) Charles Landale surveyed three possible routes. The choice fell on Newtyle, midway between Coupar Angus and Glamis. The line, which began in a tunnel some distance north of Dundee harbour, ended in a field at Newtyle, then only a small collection of dwellings. The main obstacle in the 11-mile track was the crossing of the Sidlaw hills, some 530 feet high. This meant that the line had to go up and down three fairly steep inclines. At first, no locomotive was strong enough to navigate these hills, and horses were used instead. But eventually this problem was solved by using stationary engines which were hauled up and down by rope. It took six years for the line to be completed and James McNaughton was one of those involved. In December 1831 it opened to passenger traffic. The first coaches looked like stage-coaches on rails. The first-class fare, which bought a seat inside, was one shilling and sixpence; those travelling outside paid one shilling.[15]

James had proved both trustworthy and reliable. When he heard

Probably my great-grandfather James McNaughton, in middle age.

that the line was to be extended eastwards towards Glamis and that tenders were being sought, he knew the time had come to be his own master. He was clear-sighted and growing in knowledge.[16] Even-tempered and respected by his men, he was also ambitious. He understood the vast changes that were happening to his world and was determined to be in the vanguard of this revolution from horse to steam. It was an exciting time to be alive if one had vision and stamina. James McNaughton had both.

On 14 May 1832 a meeting was held at the Angel Inn, Meigle, to gauge public interest and to attract subscribers for the 'Strathmore Railway'. The following year, on 17 June, a group of enthusiasts met at Mr Hendry's inn in Glamis. Their aim was to extend the line from Newtyle to the Market-Muir of Glamis. Shortly afterwards, an Act of Parliament authorised the 'Newtyle and Glammiss Railway' with an issued share capital of £20,000 and a loan of £6,600. The construction costs were estimated at £2,222 per mile, a low figure in those early days, and the company did not need to raise further money. This economy was due to Archibald McGlashan, the Clerk of Works, a canny Scot who managed to achieve a much tighter budget than either of the two existing lines.

The course of the proposed line was divided into five lots, and each was put out to tender. The first two lots went to John Walker and Donald Campbell, who began working from the junction with the Coupar Angus Railway, while the laying of blocks and rails and the bridging of the Dean Water and the Eassie Burn were tendered for separately. The Dean was to be crossed by a bridge of either wood or masonry with a span of 50 feet and the Burn by another with a span of 20 feet. By the beginning of June 1836, Walker and Campbell had moved about 8,400 cubic yards of material. They were the largest group working on the railway and employed 20 carts and 50 men. It had been intended to obtain earth for the embankments from one of the cuttings, which would have been made wider in consequence. But McGlashan decided to take extra soil from one of the knolls through which the line had to pass, thus reducing the width of the cutting. In this way, much money was saved.

James's bid for lot number 3, west of Eassie, was successful. Employing 80 men, many of them Irish labourers or 'navvies' (navigators), who had fled from starvation in Ireland to find work in Scotland, he used only six carts, relying on barrows to move the earth. By the end of April 1836 he had shifted 12,500 cubic yards, most of the work being done in the Myre of Ingliston.[17] Lot 4 went to Thomas Hefferon, who employed 30 men and four

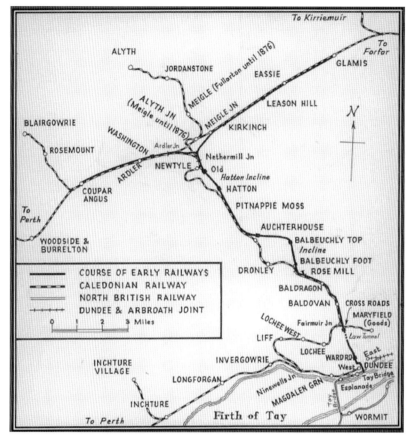

Map of the railway from Dundee to Newtyle.

carts. This stretch of the line was centred around the farms of Dunkenny and Eassie. Lastly, John McLaren and John Ballantyne took lot number 5 at the eastern end of the line. They employed only 15 men but used eight carts and by the end of April had shifted some 8,000 cubic yards of spoil, mostly in the section known as the King's Myre.

Although the winter of 1836/37 was not very cold, it was wet. Work was halted in case the newly quarried stone blocks from Pitnappie Quarry cracked in a hard frost. In February a section of the line just built west of Kirkinch village flooded. In the following months, construction continued piecemeal. In addition to the incessant rain, money was beginning to run out. The Bedlington

Iron Co. refused to supply further rails until the £1,400 debt was paid. Despite these setbacks, the line eventually opened in June 1838, the same month that the young Queen Victoria was crowned in Westminster Abbey.

Apparently, about this time, James had a liaison with a certain Jean Ramsay, daughter of Andrew Ramsay, nurseryman of Linlithgow. She gave birth to their son, William, who, although illegitimate, was mentioned in his father's will.[18] James did not marry Jean, but on 4 December 1837, at Forfar, just a month short of his 31st birthday, he wed the 17-year-old Ann Davidson. Their daughter, Susan, was born at Netherhatton, near Dunkeld, on 3 November 1838 and was baptised on 12 December. By 1841 the family, who included Joseph Davidson, perhaps Ann's brother, were living in the Polmont district of Stirling.[19] Some time later, Ann died. We do not know why, but perhaps it was in childbirth, which claimed so many lives

By this time, new railways were emerging all over Scotland. James McNaughton's reputation as a reliable contractor was well-known. He won the contract to build the railway between Glasgow and Ayr, an important undertaking, and so, shortly after Ann's death, he moved west to Ayrshire. His unmarried sister, Janet, eight years his senior, came with him as guardian to his daughter. After several years alone, on 12 March 1851 he married for the second time at the age of 44. His bride was the 34-year-old Ellen Ferrier, daughter of William Ferrier, an Edinburgh bookbinder, and his wife, Euphemia Burden.[20] Ellen was one of their seven children, the others being James, George Stratton, David, Margaret, John and Gilbert. James took his new bride home to 33 Beechwood Square, Auchinleck. Besides his daughter, now 12, the household consisted of his 52-year-old sister, and his young brother-in-law, David Ferrier, aged 28, an Edinburgh bookseller. Twenty-one-year-old Jessie Ferguson, whom he had brought with him from Caputh, was the family's only servant. Nine months later, on Christmas Day, his second daughter was born. She was baptised Euphens Ellen to distinguish her from James's mother-in-law Euphemia.

As each new piece of railroad was put out to tender, James was much in demand. In the late summer of 1853, he was working on the Glasgow to Edinburgh railway. Not wishing to leave his heavily pregnant wife behind in Auchinleck, he rented Field Cottage, Linlithgow, so that they could be together. It was there, on 27 September 1853, that the couple's first son, James John, was born. A few days later, the Reverend William Lowe, a Congregational minister, made the long journey by horse or carriage from Forfar to baptise the son of his old friend.[21]

Fifteen months later, at 3.15 in the morning of 4 January 1855 at Beechwood Square, Ellen gave birth to my grandfather. He was baptised George Ferrier Anderson McNaughton, the first two names after his mother's brother. On 26 January 1857 the family was completed with the arrival of David Norman. Again, the first Christian name chosen was that of one of his maternal uncles. The four children, and their motherless half-sister Susan, were brought up in a close and loving family, and were taught to be dutiful, truthful, and God-fearing.[22] By the time George was six, his father

The four children of James and Ellen McNaughton. L–R: Norman, Euphans, James and George.

25

decided to move from Auchinleck into a more commodious house at 36 Sandgate Street, Ayr. He was becoming increasingly prosperous, his reputation was growing, and he could afford a bigger establishment. The 1861 census shows that, besides the four children, Susan and her aunt Janet, the household now contained four servants. They were Jane Douglas, a 17-year-old Ayrshire lass; Jane Gilchrist, who came from Stirlingshire and who, at 42, was probably the cook; Grace McMurtrie, 26, born in Dalmellington, Ayrshire; and the tweenie, or maid-of-all-work, Mary Nicoll, also from Dalmellington, who at 15 was the youngest.

Ellen may have found it difficult to run such a big establishment, where her sister-in-law, a still unmarried lady of 62, had held sway for so long. Perhaps, in order to give everyone a change of scene, Ellen took her family to visit their first cousins in Edinburgh. Her brother, James, some seven years older, lived in the Old Town. In 1851, he was a struggling artist who taught drawing at the Edinburgh College of Art in order to make ends meet. He lived with his large family in Heriot Place, two minutes walk from the school. Fourteen years earlier, on 24 October 1837, he had married the young Elizabeth Stuckey, the daughter of a shoemaker from Taunton, Somerset.[23] By 1851 the four-storey house was crowded with children, his sister-in-law Rosina Stuckey, who worked as a dressmaker, and his brother, George Ferrier, an Edinburgh bookseller like his brother David. They were all looked after by Margaret Dow, a general servant, who was 20. By the time the McNaughton children were growing up, James Ferrier had become established and well-known. He and Elizabeth had seven children. His eldest daughter, born on 14 September 1838, was also named Euphemia, after his mother. Another daughter, Elizabeth, arrived two years later, on 9 April 1840. She was followed by a son, William, on 5 December, 1841; another daughter, Rosina Froom, named after her mother's sister, was born on 20 January 1844. The family was completed by three more sons: James, on 26 April 1848; George Stratton, who, like his father, would become a well-known artist, on 15 March 1852; and finally, David, born on 9 April 1854 and thus nine months older than his cousin George

McNaughton, my grandfather. The young Ferriers grew and thrived. The street outside was a quiet cul-de-sac bounded by the old city wall. Here they could play hopscotch on the cobbled stones and look up to the great mass of the Castle towering above them.

Meanwhile, their Ayrshire cousins were also growing up. On 30 April 1861, James' eldest daughter, Susan, now 22, married the Reverend Thomas Underwood, the 34-year-old minister of the parish of Irongray, Kirkcudbrightshire. A little more than a year later,

My great-great-uncle James Ferrier, artist brother of Ellen McNaughton.

on 4 August 1863, their eldest son, James McNaughton Underwood, was born at the Manse at 10.45 in the evening.

James McNaughton's reputation continued to grow and he needed a more prestigious house. By the time of the 1871 census he had moved again, this time to a substantial dwelling named Standalane in Stewarton, a town in East Ayrshire. The household was smaller now. The four house servants had been replaced by two sisters from Kilmains, Margaret and Janet Kirkwood, aged 15 and 13. They were housemaid and tablemaid respectively. Absent from the family was Aunt Janet. Perhaps she was away visiting. Now in her late sixties, she was in failing health and suffering from hardening of the arteries. After a week's illness, she died at 3.50 in the afternoon of 5 March 1874 of a pulmonary apoplexy; she was 75. Her brother, James, was absent from her bedside.

At this time, James was busy constructing the joint railway from Barrhead to Kilmarnock. Now 67 years old, he was reaching the end of his busy working life, but his reputation was assured. He had been involved in constructing all the important railways of the region: the Glasgow & Ayr, the Edinburgh & Glasgow, and the North British Railway. His contract from Paisley to Howood included the Elderslie Viaduct; some years later he built the impressive Lugar Viaduct, near Cumnock. He was regarded with affection and respect by all members of the community. By 1881, having retired from active life, he had moved again, to Roseburn House, Racecourse Road, Ayr. He was now 74. His household contained three servants. Two were Mary Craig, the 29-year-old cook from Ayr, and Jessie Dillon, a 23-year-old general servant. Now, in his old age, James employed a coachman, Hugh Fraser, who was 40 and married. James's sons were growing up. The three boys had left home, James to become an engineer and George to read theology at Glasgow University.[24] Norman was reading law in London. Euphans had married the well-to-do John Strain, a civil engineer, and lived in some splendour at Cassilis House, Maybole, 7 miles south of Ayr, which her husband rented from the Marquess of Ailsa.[25] Euphans inherited the Ferrier bookish gene and published several novels as well as contributing to newspapers and magazines.[26]

James spent his retirement giving useful service to his community. He was a regular member of the Church of Scotland, and a tolerant Conservative. He remained mentally alert and full of vigour until the last. On 9 February 1890, James's long and useful life came to an end. Enjoying a game of chess with an old friend, as was his wont, he suddenly felt faint. The doctor was called and he appeared to recover. But at nine o'clock another heart attack occurred and three hours later, at ten minutes after midnight, he died. He was 83 years old. He was buried in Ayr cemetery, and was mourned by the whole community. He was remembered as an excellent employer, respected for his 'fairness and consideration' and by the 'harmony which existed between him and his men'.[27]

During the seven lonely years that remained, his widow Ellen had the happiness of several family events. On 7 April 1891, her beloved son George married Margaret Anderson at Pollockshields Established Church, Glasgow. The following year, on 20 February 1892, she was presented with a grandson, who was named John, after his paternal great-grandfather. He was always known as Jack and was my father. Two years later, on 24 June 1894, he was joined by a brother, George Stewart Burns. Ellen moved to London to live with her lawyer son. By this time, Norman, not yet 40, had a successful practice at the Bar and was living in Burntwood Grange, a substantial house in Wandsworth. But his mother, now in her late seventies, knew that her health was failing. A diabetic for some years, she now developed kidney trouble. Following a stroke, she died on 4 June 1897 at Burntwood Grange at the age of 80.

A War Widow 1916. Jane Monteith (*née* Wilson), who introduced my parents, with her son Jack, born 2 days before his father was killed in France (see pages 93 and 102).

Notes

1. Presbyterians who bound themselves by religious and political oaths to maintain the cause of their religion. Charles I's attempt to introduce the Scottish Prayer Book prompted the National Covenant of 1638, which was very widely signed (F.L.Cross, *The Oxford Dictionary of the Christian Church*, OUP, Oxford, 1957).

2. My father's maternal grandmother, Margaret Finlayson, was the daughter of Francis Finlayson, the son of Janet Finlayson, *née* Glen, the daughter of Janet Niven (1713–17??), who married Thomas Glen in 1737, whose father William Niven (m. Margaret Shieles) was the son of William Niven, the Covenanter of Pollokshaws in the parish of Eastwood, Glasgow.

3. The Conventicle Act (1664) declared illegal all meetings in private houses of more than five people who gathered for worship other than that prescribed by the Book of Common Prayer (Cross).

4. Now a suburb of Glasgow.

5. The Test Act (1673) required all office holders under the Crown to receive the Eucharist according to the rites of the Church of England and to take the oath of allegiance to the King (Cross).

6. At the same time, Monmouth landed at Lyme, in Dorset, but his army was defeated at Sedgemoor and the rebels were savagely punished by Judge Jeffreys. Monmouth lost his head at the Tower of London in July. Argyle, too, was unsuccessful and was executed in Edinburgh in June 1685.

7. Information from Bill Johnson, Dunecht Estates, Dunnottar. (Reverend Douglas Gordon Barron, *The Castle of Dunnottar and its History*, based on Reverend Robert Woodrow, *History of the Sufferings of the Church of Scotland*, and quoted in the Dunnottar guide book.)

8. Barmagachan, built in the 17th century, is the oldest fortified house in the area. It lies 1 mile outside Kirkcudbright and faces south overlooking the Solway firth. The McLellans also owned Kirkcudbright castle.

9. The story of William Niven was written by my great-great uncle Francis Finlayson and based on Reverend Robert Woodrow, *The Sufferings of the Kirk of Scotland* (also known as *Woodrow's Church History*). I found it in an old tin trunk and wrote an article for *The Scotsman* (9 July 1960).

10. OPR 344/1-4 Dowally BMD.

11. Dowally – Births FR 026.6.

12. Information from Jane Anderson, archivist at Blair Castle.

13. Scots name for a farmstead.

14. John, 7th Duke of Atholl, *Chronicles of the Atholl and Tullibardine Families*, 5 vols, Edinburgh, Ballantyne Press, 1908.

15. It was one of the earliest railways, which obtained its Act of Parliament before Stephenson's *Rocket* ran at the Rainhill Trials and opened only six months after the Liverpool & Manchester Railway (Niall Ferguson, *The Dundee and Newtyle Railway*, Oakwood Press, Oxford 1995 – The Oakwood Library of Railway History).

16. From his obituary in the *Ayr Advertiser*, 13 February 1890.

17. Niall Ferguson, *The Dundee and Newtyle Railway*.

30

[18] Information from my second cousin, Donald McNaughton.

[19] Information from Donald McNaughton.

[20] The Ferriers were a literate and literary family. One member was Susan Ferrier, the celebrated 18th-century novelist. Euphemia's parents, who married in 1776, were probably James Burden, a hairdresser, and Margaret Clerk. See Appendix 1, page 127.

[21] James John married Jane McLeod and had four children – James Colin, Erick Colin Hicks, Jane Colin (known as Sheena) and Ronald McLeod Colin. Erick married Lena Stewart in 1925; they had Derick, who died aged 44 in 1975, and Hamish who is the father of Donald, Iain Stewart and Norman Eric. Jane Colin married Reginald Webb at a service performed by my grandfather. Ronald was killed in a motor-bike accident in September 1914 on his way to enlist.

[22] I have in my possession a book called *The Children's Picture Gallery – Engravings from One Hundred Paintings by Eminent English Artists adapted for the Young*. It is inscribed 'From Mamma to her darling Son, George Ferrier Anderson McNaughton, June 18th 1861'. At this time he was nearly six and a half years old.

[23] They were married in the parish of Buccleuch, Edinburgh, by the Reverend Dr Patrick Clason.

[24] There seems to have been a split between James and his siblings after the First World War. Although my father was close to his cousins, the children of Norman and Euphans, I do not remember any mention of James's family.

[25] My cousin John Hawkesworth remembered 'rather frightening royal visits' to Cassilis (pronounced 'Cassels') as a child: 'A big granite Scottish baronial sort of house on a bend in the Doon. Thick walls and winding staircases. All on our best behaviour.'

[26] Their children were Laurence, a barrister; Helen (Nell) who married an eminent engineer, A.K. Wolfe-Barry, the son of Sir John Barry, engineer of Tower Bridge and grandson of Sir Charles Barry, architect of the Houses of Parliament; and Hilary who married Harold Wyllie, the artist son of W. L. Wyllie.

[27] From his obituary in the *Ayr Advertiser*, 13 February 1890.

My great-great-grandfather James Kitson I, pioneer engine-builder and Mayor of Leeds 1860–62.

Chapter 2

The Kitson Dynasty 1807–1911

'And here an engine fit for my proceeding'

The Two Gentlemen of Verona 3.1.138

My mother, the Hon. Doris Claire Kitson, was the third of the seven daughters of the second Baron Airedale, and her background was very different from my father's. The Kitsons, although titled, came from humble but gifted stock. The founder of the dynasty was her great-grandfather James, who was born at seven o'clock in the morning of 27 October 1807 in the Brunswick Tavern,[1] Camp Road, Leeds, where his father, William,[2] was the publican. When William died of alcoholism aged 37, his 16-year-old son had to help his mother, Hannah,[3] untie the muddled affairs of her husband, run the business and care for five younger children.[4]

Few would have guessed that this handsome young man, who slept, it was said, under the bar of his father's inn,[5] would become an engineering genius and that his progeny would become famous as politicians, artists and academics. Square-shouldered, jaunty and physically strong, James was determined to make his way in the world. He helped his mother in the tavern and worked in a local dyeworks, where he was injured. Undeterred, he joined the newly formed Mechanics' Institute and Literary Society where he was noticed as a 'diligent student in drawing and mathematical classes'.[6] This was a time when the first locomotives were appearing and the relative merits of rail and canal were hotly disputed. There was much opposition from those who thought rail was unsafe and that people would be suffocated going through tunnels or travelling at 30mph. Rail was considered more economical than canals when 'a celerity of four miles an hour'[7] was required. James was much influenced by a book called *A Practical Treatise on Railroads,* written in

1825 by Nicholas Wood, a colliery engineer. The young man's imagination was fired and, like my paternal great-grandfather, he realised that this was the new revolution.[8]

On 13 September 1828, at Leeds Parish Church, a few weeks before his 21st birthday, James made a shrewd marriage. Although Ann Newton's father was the owner of 'a leading firm of painters and decorators', her mother's family were people of substance.[9] The marriage produced eleven children.[10] Four sons (Frederick, James, John and Arthur) and two daughters (Mary and Emily) grew to adulthood; the remaining four sons and one daughter died in infancy. At that time, when knowledge of hygiene was rudimentary and contraception unheard of, large families were necessary in order to produce living children.

In 1835, now intent on becoming an engineer, James moved to Hunslet, south of the river Aire, to be nearer the engineering shops where the fascinating new locomotives were built.[11] Two years later, he became the junior in a partnership with two others, David Laird, a farmer with capital, and Charles Todd.[12] To their surprise, being an unknown firm and before they had even found their own premises, they received an order from the Liverpool & Manchester Railway for six locomotives. James began work on the first. Soon crowds arrived, among them the great Robert Stephenson,[13] to see this crazy young man who was building his engine at one end of a weaving shed with a weaver at work at the other. A single small door served as the exit, so people asked how he was going to get the engine out. James kept silent. When the time came he knocked down a wall and the little engine rolled out to the astonishment of the scoffers.[14] Soon afterwards, Todd, a difficult man, dropped out to set up on his own, and in 1839 Kitson and Laird established the Airedale Foundry.[15]

This was a boom time for the railways. In 1838 there were 490 miles of track in England and Wales, of which 200 were opened that year.[16] James Kitson prospered. At the Airedale Foundry, he began making locomotives which would travel all over the world. Almost 6,000 engines were built for 48 railway companies at home and 80 companies in 28 countries abroad.[17] In 1854 James

My great-great-grandmother, Ann Kitson.

Her mother, my great-great-great-grandmother Ann Newton.

My great-great-grandfather James Kitson I *c* 1860.

bought Monkbridge Ironworks, which manufactured weldless iron tyres for railway engines. His two oldest sons, Fred and James, were appointed to run it.[18]

Besides developing his engineering skills, James soon established himself as a leading citizen. From 1860 to 1862 he served two terms as Mayor of Leeds; to be elected for a second term was an unprecedented honour. In addition, he was a Director of the North Eastern Railway and Chairman of the Yorkshire Banking Company, later the Midland Bank and now HSBC. In 1864, as Chairman, he laid the foundation stone of the new Leeds infirmary.

James was very musical and, like his older daughter Mary, he had a fine voice. In his youth he had built an organ in an outhouse

Three Kitson locomotives.

of his father's inn, and he was one of the founders of the Leeds Music Festival, which still exists. His interests were wide. From 1856 to 1869 he was a member of the Conversation Club, a gathering of professional men, and the subjects on which he led discussion illustrate the breadth of his thought: 'the shortening of penal servitude'; 'English policy towards China'; 'whether fine arts or industrial arts should take precedence in an exhibition'. This was no parochial mind.

Religion was important. Although James had been brought up Anglican, and sang in the choir

Kitson tram engine.

at the parish church where his first six children were baptised, in 1840 he succumbed to the forceful teaching of the Reverend Charles Wicksteed, the Minister of Mill Hill Chapel, in Leeds City Square. Crossing the floor from Anglicanism to Unitarianism was a big leap, and was considered a 'leg-down' socially by some of his more snobbish relations.[19] The strong faith that he found at Mill Hill Chapel would influence both himself and his second son.

In 1865, Ann Newton died. A kindly woman of 'charm and character'[20] and remembered as 'Dear Mrs Kitson', she was buried, as an Anglican, in Roundhay churchyard. She too, had come a long way from her father's decorating business, and when her husband was Mayor had given 'splendid dinner parties for the barristers on circuit'.[21]

37

By the early 1860s, when James had gained civic distinction, it was time for him to establish himself as a country gentleman. In 1868, he paid £17,000 for Elmet Hall, a substantial property near the village of Roundhay, on rising ground some 3 miles north of Leeds.[22] He demolished the old neo-classical mansion erected in 1815 and built an Italianate villa with superb views over the town. There could be no doubt that this was the home of a successful self-made man. The magnificent panelling, mahogany doors, the great hall and two grand staircases were all designed to impress.

The surrounding parkland was acquired for the citizens by Leeds Town Council in 1871, a scheme strongly opposed by James, who feared that the hoi-polloi would peer over his walls and that 'unseemly behaviour' would occur – a snobbish view from one born in a tavern. Despite his protests, the scheme went ahead and Roundhay Park soon became an established recreation place for the people of Leeds.[23] (I remember being taken there for walks. To my childish eyes, it was a magical place, with rushing waterfalls and narrow hidden paths beside a foaming stream.)

Now that he had a suitable house, James married again. The chief bridesmaid at his daughter May's marriage to Edwin Clark in 1865 was Elizabeth Hutchinson, the 32-year-old daughter of the vicar of East Stoke, Nottinghamshire. She caught James's eye. He decided that she would make an excellent second wife, and three

Elmet Hall, Roundhay, from the south-west in about 1880.

years later he married her. Marriage to one of Leeds' most prosperous citizens, even one so much older, must have been a considerable coup for the impecunious parson's family. James, now 61, had lost none of his virility. Although his wife was not in her first youth, he fathered four more children, the youngest, Annette, born when he was 66.

In 1883 James became seriously ill with a clot on his brain. For two years he was looked after by two male nurses, and Elizabeth, now 50, had to supervise the vast house, with its eight gardeners, coachman and groom,

James Kitson I aged about 60 – self-made and proud.

and large indoor staff, including a butler and footmen. Eventually, on 30 June 1885, James died, much lamented by the people of Leeds and unaware of the lustre that his second son would bring to the name of Kitson. That son recalled: 'He was what the French call "*grand industriel*" and a most tender parent. He and I have been through some trying work together for thirty years without a shadow of unkindness. He has been... the instrument for the development of many social blessings in his native town.'[24]

* * *

All except one of the six children of James's first family, achieved, or married, eminence. The youngest became embroiled in a scandal that seriously damaged both a brother and a sister.[25]

The eldest, Frederick William, born in 1829, 'thoroughly Yorkshire in speech and manner',[26] inherited his father's engineering flair. It was to him that James entrusted the running of the Airedale Foundry, and it was his genius that ensured the continuing success of the firm. His bride was Ellen Talbot,[27] who gave him three sons:

39

My great-great-uncle John Hawthorn Kitson, *c* 1880, and, opposite, his wife Jessie Kitson, *c* 1885.

Frederick James, born in 1861; George Talbot, born in 1864; and Henry Herbert, who arrived seven years later. Their first child was a daughter, Ellen, who was born in 1858. (I remember her as a charming old lady of about 70, Aunt Nelly, who wore a narrow black velvet band round her neck.) Frederick William died in 1877, aged only 48. For the previous five years he had been afflicted by 'rheumatic gout' and on 25 November he succumbed to pneumonia. This was a disaster for the firm, for by this time his father was seriously ill. Later, two of Fred's sons, Frederick James and Henry Herbert, took over, and despite the loss of its guiding spirit the firm prospered.[28]

John Hawthorn Kitson,[29] James's third son by his first marriage, inherited Elmet.[30] There appears to have been some flaw in his character. His elder brother James thought that, although he had 'intellectual powers of a high order', there was 'some strain... which darkened his career'.[31] This enigmatic reference presumably means that he drank – he gave 'an impression of oddity and unreliability'.[32] Despite these shortcomings, he was a renowned Alpinist and was elected a member of the Alpine Club when he was only 24 – a rare honour. However, his love of liquor overcame him, and on Whit Sunday, 21 May 1899, he was found by his footman lying flat on his face in the dining-room. He had apparently had a cerebral stroke while reaching for a whisky bottle, and died shortly afterwards. He was 56.

John Hawthorn married Jessie Ellershaw, and had three gifted children: Robert, born in 1873, Ethel (1875) and Beatrice (1877). Jessie, although described as 'a very widowy person', looks forthright and intelligent in the photograph opposite. After

40

her husband's death, she remained at Elmet.

Like my mother and her sisters, John and Jessie's children were left in the care of brutal nurses during their parents' frequent absences. One enjoyed a tipple at the local pub and was in the habit of drugging Robert, probably with opium, to keep him quiet. Fortunately, he survived. Beatrice was a noisy child and the nurse would take her by the heels and bang her head on the floor until she bit her tongue. Presumably this had the desired effect.[33]

Having survived these childhood horrors, Robert Hawthorn, now an excessively handsome young man with piercing blue eyes, went up to Trinity College, Cambridge. Here he gained a First in Natural Sciences. He dutifully entered the Kitson family firm, but his heart was not in engineering – it was in art.

Like most rich people, the Kitsons wintered abroad, and in 1898 they ventured to Sicily to try out the new coastal railway. At Taormina, a small town perched on a steep hill, Robert had secret meetings with Baron von Gloeden, a noted photographer of young men. Although almost unknown, Taormina was slowly becoming a homosexual's paradise, not least because of von Gloeden.[34] Robert was stunned by its beauty. He knew he was homosexual and realised that he had reached his nirvana. He determined to spend his life in this magical place. When his father died the following year, he came into enough money to fulfil his destiny. While he was at Cambridge, he had contracted rheumatic fever after falling into the frozen river Cam. England, after the trial of Oscar Wilde a few years earlier, was riddled with homophobia and no place to admit one was homosexual. His poor health was reason enough for Robert's move to Sicily.

The arrival in Taormina of this fair young man with the face of Adonis proved a sensation. Soon, a band of handsome acolytes, many of them models of von Gloeden, gathered around him. Robert's aim now was to build a house. He found the ideal place, high on the hillside above the town and below the Greek amphitheatre, with breathtaking views of Mount Etna. The locals thought he was mad to choose somewhere fit only for 'pigs and peasants'.[35] But Don Roberto, as he was known, persisted, and gradually his house – which he called *Casa Cuseni* – took shape. As an engineer, he knew all about building in difficult places, but the site he had chosen caused many problems. Every scrap of material had to be brought up from the town below, much of it on mules or carried on the heads of the local women. Apart from ancient Greek wells, there was no water – again, every drop had to be transported. As an artist, he was determined that his terraced garden should be the envy of all.

The house took three years to build but, at last, in 1907, it was finished. Robert filled the handsome *salone* with precious artefacts and asked his former tutor and sometime lover,[36] the noted artist Frank Brangwyn, to paint murals for the dining-room. This was the height of the Arts and Crafts movement, and Brangwyn also designed the dining-room furniture. Many flocked to see this amazing house, and *Casa Cuseni* was coveted by all.

All this time, Robert had been painting scenes of incredible beauty. Watercolour was his medium, and the pictures he produced are still stunning today.[37] Although he described himself as an 'amateur', others thought differently. It was said that 'there are many painters in Taormina, but Bob Kitson is the only artist.'[38] He was a fulfilled and happy man.

Robert did not forget his native city. In 1912 he suggested that Brangwyn should decorate the apse of the newly built St Aidan's church in Roundhay, where his brother-in-law, the Reverend Arthur Swayne, was the incumbent. After many difficulties, the artist designed a most beautiful mosaic which is still one of the glories of Leeds.

Robert Kitson continued to live in Taormina, often wintering in

My great-uncle Robert Hawthorn Kitson aged about 25.

Casa Cuseni, the house Robert Kitson built at Taormina, Sicily.

North Africa, where he produced many lovely watercolours. But the Second World War destroyed this life, and he returned to England. Afterwards he was determined to go back to his beloved house. In 1946 he became the first foreign resident to return to Taormina, but his time there was shortlived and he died the following year at the age of 74. *Casa Cuseni* was left to his niece, Daphne Phelps, whose evocative book, *A House in Sicily*, continues this story.

Robert's sister, Ethel, who had the same piercing blue eyes, was a young woman of formidable intelligence who gained a place at Newnham College, Cambridge, at a time when women were rarely educated to this level. Brought up in the Liberal circles of her Uncle James, she was a powerful advocate of the underdog. When she left Newnham in 1898, she was the only woman of her year to be awarded the equivalent of a First Class degree.[39] Soon afterwards, she married Murray Phelps, a solicitor from Edgbaston, Birmingham. Like many of his generation, he was traumatised by

his First World War experiences and was afterwards unable to work in his chosen profession.

A Courtyard in Morocco, watercolour by Robert Kitson.

Ethel and her sister Beatrice were very different. Considered delicate as a child, Beatrice received a paltry education from half-illiterate governesses, though she probably possessed as good a brain as her sister. She never married but formed a close friendship with Ethel Mallinson, a well-known local artist.[40] Despite her poor education, Beatrice was one of Leeds' first women magistrates and in 1942 became the City's first female Lord Mayor.

* * *

'Don Roberto' (Robert Kitson) at *Casa Cuseni*.

When James Kitson died in 1885, his widow Elizabeth, like many dowagers before her, had to move out of Elmet Hall to allow her step-son, John Hawthorn, to move in. Where was she to go? She and her four children rented South Luffen-ham Hall, a lovely Queen Anne house near Stamford. She was not short of money, for her husband had left £80,000 – the equivalent of several millions today. But soon the bailiffs called, for the landlord owed money, and they were off again. This time the choice was Sussex, and they lived for a time in St Leonard's. Later, she had the fore-sight to live in Cambridge where her children moved in intellectual circles and made advantageous marriages.

But in 1895 tragedy struck. Her brilliant eldest son, Reggie, who had excelled at Cambridge, became ill with a brain tumour. A horrendous operation, in which parts of his brain and skull were removed, failed to save him. His family was told that the chance of him surviving with-out being paralysed, both mentally and physically, was highly unlikely.[41] He died on 31 January, aged 26. It was a grievous blow.

April garden at *Casa Cuseni* looking towards Mount Etna.

Elizabeth's second son (and James Kitson's tenth), Sydney Decimus, was some-thing of a maverick. Expelled from Charterhouse, he never-theless went up to Trinity College, Cambridge. Trained as an architect, and in his

46

The *salone* at *Casa Cuseni*.

opinion not a very good one, he enjoyed telling *risqué* stories which shocked his sisters. He married Winifred Tetley, of the brewing family, and their joint incomes kept them in comfort for life. His great claim to fame is as the biographer of John Sell Cotman, whose watercolours he collected.[42] He died of tuberculosis in 1937, living just long enough to see his *magnum opus*, *The Life of John Sell Cotman*, published by Faber & Faber in that year.

Daphne Phelps, Robert Kitson's niece, in the gardens of *Casa Cuseni*, whose history she later wrote.

Sydney's two sisters were very different. The older, Eva, was large and bossy and bullied her mild-mannered husband, the

47

Professor Edwin Charles
Clark, Regius Professor of
Civil Law at the University
of Cambridge; portrait by
Philip de Laszlo.

Sydney Decimus
Kitson.

Reverend Arthur Swayne. A bridge
fanatic, whose post-mortems after
the game were terrifying, she
smoked 50 Passing Clouds a day.
Surprisingly, she did not die of
lung cancer (although her white
hair did become stained with
nicotine), but of dropsy in her 80s,
'all her volcanic energy dissipated
with age'.[43]

The younger sister, Annette,
born in 1873, was quite unlike her
sibling. Although shy and retiring
when young, she was clever and
later became a suffragette, a Poor
Law Guardian and a good public

speaker. In 1910, when she was 37, she married, as his second wife, Sir John Matthews, Chief Justice of the Supreme Court of the Bahamas. Their son, Brian, a schoolmaster at Uppingham, has written an interesting family memoir. His sister, Esther, married David Tate of the sugar family.

Elizabeth Kitson's two stepdaughters both married distinguished men. Mary Anne, or May, chose Edwin Charles Clark, who later became Regius Professor of Civil Law at Cambridge. Their son was Edwin Kitson Clark, Chairman of Kitson and Co., author of *The Kitsons of Leeds*, and the father of two sons, Edwin Bidder Clark, a Royal Navy commander, and George Kitson Clark, Fellow of Trinity College, Cambridge and a noted historian.

Emily's life was more contentious. She married the royal gynaecologist, William Playfair, *accoucheur* to the Duchess of Edinburgh and the Duchess of Connaught. He was caught up in a notorious libel case involving his sister-in-law Linda which almost destroyed his career and prevented him receiving an honour.

Linda Kitson was the wife of the youngest of James Kitson's sons, Arthur, known in the family as 'the one we don't mention'[44] – rather unfairly, as what followed was hardly his fault. This young

Ethel Kitson with fellow-students at Newnham College, Cambridge, in 1898. Ethel is in the centre, looking straight ahead.

man, who worked for the family firm, was sent to Australia where locomotives were becoming big business. In 1881 he married there Linda Leroy, who gave him two children, Arthur and Irene. Whether the marriage was unhappy we do not know, but several years later she arrived in England alone. Having some sort of gynaecological problem, she went to see her eminent brother-in-law, Dr William Playfair. He found evidence of an abortion and concluded that it must have been after she had left her husband. Being a typically moral Victorian, he was outraged and forbade his wife to have anything to do with this dissolute relation. In turn Linda Kitson sued Playfair for professional misconduct. The case, which came to court in 1896, riveted England. Many eminent doctors supported Playfair's view that it was his duty to protect his family from 'unchastity'. But public opinion turned against him and asserted that medical confidentiality towards a patient was paramount. The jury agreed, and Linda Kitson was awarded £12,000 in damages, the largest settlement for libel and slander in a British court.[45] The man who picked up most of the bill for his brother-in-law was Sir James Kitson. On his return home, Arthur set up a successful business in Stamford making pressure oil lighting systems, including those for Trinity House lighthouses. He died in Tunbridge Wells in 1915 and was referred to as 'the scourge of the Kitsons', though one feels this was unjustified.[46]

William and Emily's son became the well-known actor-manager, Sir Nigel Playfair, who made his name with a famous revival of *The Beggar's Opera* in the 1920s. He managed the Lyric Theatre, Hammersmith, and was knighted in 1928. He died in 1934 aged 60.

* * *

It was James Kitson's second son, also James, who honed and polished the Kitson name. Born in his father's tavern, the Brunswick, on 22 September 1835, he was welcomed into a close and loving family and educated at West Riding Proprietary School in Wakefield. Places at Oxford and Cambridge were closed to dissenters (as James's father had become in 1840). So young James

Portrait of Mrs
William Playfair
(Emily Kitson) by
John Singer Sargent,
1887.

was fortunate to enter University College London, which did not
apply such restrictions. Here he read chemistry and natural
sciences. And here he met Grosvenor Talbot, who became his close
friend and later his brother-in-law.[47]

All four of James Kitson's sons by his first marriage were put
into 'The Works' – but it was the two eldest, Frederick William and
James, who inherited their father's engineering genius. Like his
father, his faith meant much to young James, and for 14 years he
taught in the Chapel Sunday School. Many of the leading Leeds

51

My great-grand-father James Kitson II, aged about 40.

manufacturing families had become Unitarians – the Luptons, the Cliffs and the Schuncks among others. One of the teachers was a serious-minded girl called Emily Cliff. James decided make her his wife and they were married at the Mill Hill Chapel in 1860.

The Cliffs were extremely rich – even richer than the Kitsons. Emily's father, Joseph, had made his fortune in the firebrick industry. He got off the mark earlier than the Kitsons, building a large house on a hill at Wortley in 1842. Money was his god.[48] A young

52

visitor taken to tea in the very fine drawing room asked if one of the gilt chairs was 'all gold'. 'Oh, no my dear,' said Mrs Cliff,[49] 'we should soon have turned it into guineas if it was.' This reply amazed the girl, who never forgot it.[50]

Mrs James Kitson (Emily Cliff) in her 30s.

Her daughter was of different mettle. Emily Cliff was one of the outstanding women of her generation and, had she lived, would have taken her place among the great Victorian women educationalists such as Dorothea Beale and Frances Buss.[51] Emily was not only rich but highly intelligent and imbued with the same spirit of philanthropy as her husband. Almost at once, seeing all round her desperate poverty and lack of education, she determined to improve the lives of the local women. She taught herself the rudiments of hygiene and cookery and gave a series of lectures called 'Sanitary Lessons' and 'Papers on Practical Cookery'. Her notes can be seen today.[52] She asked eminent professors from Leeds University to visit and they supplied her with accurate models of the human body with which to illustrate her lectures.

On their marriage, Emily and James lived at number 1 Hanover Square, Leeds, and there her first three children were born: Albert Ernest, my grandfather, in 1863; James Clifford in 1864; and Emily in 1866. As James became more prosperous they moved to a larger house, Spring Bank in Headingley, where Hilda was born in 1872 and Edward in September 1873.

In the intervals between bearing children, James and Emily travelled abroad where James's business interests were broadening. In 1868, they travelled to St Petersburg and Moscow, of which Emily wrote a fascinating account in her diary.[53]

There was no presentiment, in the summer of 1873, when Emily was heavily pregnant, of the coming disaster. She and James were in Salzburg from where, on 16 June, she wrote to the seven-year-old Emily (then called Amy): '... If I knew the length of Baby's feet, I would bring her some new shoes. Can she walk yet or does she never try?' Baby was Hilda, then about a year old.[54]

Soon they were back in Leeds, and on 29 September, at Spring Bank, Emily gave birth to Edward. He was her fifth child and all appeared normal. But very soon the dreaded signs of puerperal peritonitis occurred. In the days before antibiotics, there was little doctors could do to halt the infection, and James Kitson experienced the agony of watching his beloved wife die. She succumbed on 6 October, just a week later, aged 36. She, who had done so much to teach the local women about the dangers of poor hygiene and septicaemia, herself became a victim. As 'Little Bob', the stable boy at Wortley recalled, 'She was the Flower of the Family.'[55]

For James, it was a devastating blow. His political career was just taking off and Emily, who shared so many of his hopes, would have been his greatest support. As it was, he was left with five young children, the oldest of whom, Albert, must have celebrated a miserable 10th birthday just three days later. Emily was buried in Roundhay churchyard and her stricken husband threw his bunch of roses into the open grave 'as though the last of his life had gone'.[56] Emily's sister Clara and her husband Grosvenor Talbot, James's old college friend, were lifelines. They tended the grieving man and cared for his children. Talbot recalled later, 'he practically lived here for months.' In the spring of the following year, his father took James to Paris for a change of scene. His refuge was work, and he became increasingly prominent in the industrial and political life of Leeds.

Four years later, James suffered another body blow with the death of his older brother Fred, a gifted engineer who was in charge at Monkbridge. In addition to his burgeoning political life, James had to take on the running of 'The Works'. In 1880 James was elected President of the Leeds Liberal Association and in the same year was instrumental in securing the Leeds seat for William

Ewart Gladstone. (As Gladstone had just won the Midlothian election, he vacated Leeds in favour of his son, Herbert, who became a close friend of the Kitson family.)

But James was resilient. His precept was 'never look back', and in 1881 he decided to marry again. The 27-year-old Laura Fisher Smith, who had been reared in the upper echelons of Liberal society, seemed to be an astute choice for a rising politician, for Edward, Laura's father, was agent to the Earl of Dudley. James needed not only a mother for his five children, but a wife who understood his political aspirations and who would act as hostess in his increasingly social life. On 6 March 1881, he wrote to Herbert Gladstone: 'I believe I have found my true help mate. She is handsome, well bred and all I could possibly desire. I am very happy in my treasure.'[57]

At first, all seemed well. A son, Roland, was born in 1882. In June of that year, a month before his birth, James wrote again to Herbert Gladstone, who had been his best man: 'It is a year since you started me on my happy journey which has been happier than I ever hoped or deserved.'[58] With education, money and ambition, and a wife chosen for her breeding and political connections, he intended to make his mark not merely on the local stage, but on the national as well. The first essential for every up-and-coming man was a power-base, a country house where he could entertain the older landed gentry. Just before his father's death in 1885, when he was 48, he bought Gledhow Hall, some 3 miles north of Leeds, built by Carr of York, the 18th-century architect.[59] Why did he not move to Elmet? Probably Mrs James wanted a house of her own and not one that was second-hand, and with step-mother-in-law *in situ*.

Early in June, when his father was close to death, James wrote to Emily, now 19: 'I want... to tell you about your room at Gledhow which is now nearly finished.... I found the old marble fire place was cracked... so I allowed Mr Heaton to put in a new tiled hearth and an old fashioned wood mantel .... It looks so pretty. ... Mother... is a little better and is sleeping well but she will require to rest for a long time before she regains her strength.'[60] This suggests that his wife had had a miscarriage. (It must have been hard for the children to learn to call a complete stranger by that beloved name.)

Gledhow Hall, just north of Leeds, in about 1890.

The following year, 1886, he was made a Baronet and in March 1887 the new Lady Kitson gave him a daughter, Olive. But his pleasure at receiving the honour was tempered by the knowledge that his marriage was crumbling. Here and there we have tantalising snippets of life at Gledhow. In February 1886 Mrs Kitson declared, 'I can be very nasty when I try.'[61] Then, in November 1887, Albert told Emily: 'I do wish you were at home again as I am afraid her Ladyship has been putting out the Governor again. She is a fiend... an example of what a high marriage leads to without love.'[62]

Soon afterwards, Laura Kitson left James and her two young children. The sense of humiliation and failure that this proud man endured cannot be imagined. The scandal rocked Leeds. Such a step was almost unheard of in Victorian society – usually wives suffered in silence. In drawing rooms and servants' halls, tongues wagged. 'Why had she left him?' 'Was she bored with her much older husband?' 'Were his sexual demands excessive?' 'Did she fall out with her forceful step-daughter?' 'Was Olive Sir James's child?' We shall probably never know, but we assume she took a lover.[63] Certainly Olive's birth was not registered by her father, as Roland's had been, but by her mother.[64] Afterwards James referred to this time in his life as the 'fiery trial'.

56

Roland Kitson and his sister Olive in 1891 aged nine and four.

Roland Dudley,
3rd Baron
Airedale.

By May 1888 Lady Kitson was in London, and the following year, on 2 June, Hilda wrote to Emily: 'I was grieved to hear that the children are leaving you. You will miss them so much and poor father, what will he do without Olive. It seems so horrid to be so near to them and... to be so far separated. ... I wonder if I should see them in the streets if I went to London.'[65] But James did not lose his children. We do not know how long they stayed with their

58

mother, but Gledhow remained their home. There is a charming photograph[66] of the nine-year-old Roland holding the hand of his sister, who is sitting straight-backed on a high chair. She looks at the world warily, as well she might, having been deserted by her mother at so young an age.

In July, 1889 Catherine Gladstone, the Prime Minister's wife, wrote to James congratulating him on Albert's betrothal to Florence Schunck: '...May [this] bring comfort and happiness to you who, alas, needs it so much. May I be allowed to say, from my Husband and myself, how deeply we have both felt for you in all the trial and distress which has fallen upon you! And how glad we should be to be able to comfort you.'[67]

There are few references to Lady Kitson after this time. James did not divorce her, though he had every reason to do so. In 1907 he was raised to the peerage as Lord Airedale. Two years later, when he 'moved the Address' at the State Opening of Parliament, he caustically observed to Emily 'I wonder if the Peeress was at the Opening.' On James's death in 1911, she became known as 'the Dowager'. I had no idea, in my childhood, that there was another 'Lady Airedale' besides my grandmother. It seems that Laura did leave him for another man, for in 1909, when James was cruising in the liner *Omuz*, he wrote: 'A lady on board remarked to me that Lady Airedale has gone to South America. She has a son in Buenos Ayres [sic].' She died in 1939 of a stroke when she was living at Stonor House, at Steep, just outside Petersfield, afterwards the home of her daughter, Olive.

Of all James Kitson's four sons, Laura's son Roland was the one who inherited the Kitson genes. His First World War service was courageous, and he was awarded the Distinguished Service Order and the Military Cross. At the early age of 41, when he was a director of the North Eastern Railway, he was appointed a director of the Bank of England. It was, as *The Times* said 'of more than passing interest'.[68] Five years later, he became one of the original directors of the Ford Motor Company in Britain; he was appointed Chairman in 1948. In 1913 he married Sheila Vandeleur, by whom he had a son, Oliver, and a daughter, Verona. After Sheila's death in 1933 he married Christabel Pelly, a widow. I remember Roland as a tall, distinguished man, every inch a lord, and his wife as a tall, elegant woman. They were kind to me during the war. He and my father were good friends, and it infuriated my mother that he agreed to be Jack's best man at his wedding to Nancy in 1947.

On Roland's death in 1958 Oliver became the 4th Lord Airedale. Sadly, I never knew him but apparently he was a kind and gentle man of the old school. He made the House of Lords, where he was a Deputy Speaker for many years, his life and was said to be a great advertisement for the hereditary peerage. He never married. On his death in 1996 the Barony became extinct. It seems that his sister, Verona, whom again I never knew, was a delightful woman and a keen rider to hounds; she became President of the Riding for the Disabled Association. She died unmarried in 2000. Brother and sister apparently had a very unhappy childhood and Verona often cried herself to sleep; their mother, Sheila Vandeleur, was said to dislike children. [69]

Roland's sister, Olive, whom I met only once, is described by Talbot Griffith as 'one of the most charming and greatest ladies I have ever met'.[70] Her half-sisters, Emily and Hilda, were devoted to her, as they were to Roland. In 1926, at the age of 39, she married Brigadier Harold Kingsley, and inherited Stonor House, Steep, near Petersfield from her mother in 1939.[71]

Clifford Kitson as a handsome young man aged about 23.

James's son Clifford is the one we know least about. Like Emily, he inherited outstanding good looks; a photograph of him taken with the thin and weedy Albert, when both were in their early 20s, bears this out. There is a mystery about Clifford – he disappears from this story and little more is heard of him. Like his Uncle Arthur, 'he is the one we don't mention.' It was said that he became addicted to opium[72] and was exiled to Skye, where he lodged in the home of Doctor Donald Dewar. But one shaft of light appears in a letter: 'Lady Kitson was the only one who encouraged Clifford's artistic talent, and if she had been about, things might have been different.'[73] This suggests that, like his first cousin Robert Hawthorn, Clifford was a talented artist and possibly homosexual, and may explain, in the context of Victorian England, his addiction to opium and his self-exile to Skye. Clearly, he had displeased his father, for Clifford was left only £25,000, a quarter of the legacies left to his brothers – even so, not a small sum, about £1,750,000 today.[74]

By the time of her stepmother's flight in 1888, Emily, was a beautiful girl of 22, and the pet of her doting father. She at once took over the running of the house, farm and estate. A young woman of character, she kept both siblings and servants in check, standing no nonsense. Sir James, as he had become in 1886, was a generous host, entertaining the gentry, political friends and workers from his foundry at large luncheon and tea parties. In the absence of her stepmother, Emily was an excellent, if forbidding, hostess. Her housekeeping book for 1889 is evidence of the scale of their entertaining.[75] That year, her father entertained 60 foremen from Monkbridge and Airedale to a sit-down meal on the lawn. They consumed 46 lb of salmon, 17 chickens, 5 tongues, 17lb of sirloin, 12 lb of ham, 60 fruit tarts, and 207 bread rolls at a total cost of £14 18 shillings and 3 pence. They drank eleven bottles of hock, sixteen of claret, five of sherry and seven of whisky. (It is interesting that beer is not mentioned.)

Sir James's private entertaining was also lavish. There were frequent dinner parties for 16 guests and balls for 250. There were also many dances and fancy dress parties for the five young people who lived at Gledhow. There were bachelor parties, tennis and picnic parties and that staple of Victorian life, weekend house parties. During the triennial Music Festival, up to nine guests would stay for a week.

Herbert Gladstone was a frequent visitor to Gledhow, lured, no doubt, by Emily's presence.[76] Although she was very pretty and intelligent, she apparently spurned his advances. Marriage to a former Prime Minister's son would have been a considerable coup.[77] But Emily decided otherwise. Her job as her father's hostess was more important. It is not surprising that such a beautiful young woman had many suitors. One described her as 'the loveliest thing I ever saw'. In 1893, when she was 27, Emily was presented at Court by Mrs Gladstone, Herbert's mother. No expense was spared on her dress, which was garlanded with rosebuds. It must have cost thousands of pounds. Round her neck she wore a superb diamond necklace. There are impassioned letters in the Leeds archives from Henry Fisher Smith, presumably her stepmother's brother. But his pleas to take her on the river, or for her to meet him at the station, were ignored. Other admirers were rejected, and she remained a spinster, enjoying the power and celebrity of being a political hostess. There is a hint that she may have been jilted in matrimony, perhaps a latter-day Miss Havisham,[78] for she possessed a most beautiful bridal veil of Brussels lace. When Enid, rather tactlessly, wrote to her before Margaret's wedding in 1949 to ask if she could borrow 'the family veil', she received a curt rebuff: 'It is *not* the "family" veil – it is *my* veil.'[79]

Emily controlled her step-siblings as well as the servants. On one occasion, Olive, who was about six years old, came late to luncheon. Emily wrinkled her nose: 'I detect a strange aroma,' she said. The child confessed that she had fallen into a dung heap.[80]

There was little scope for Victorian women to use their brains. But Emily had inherited her mother's intellect and philanthropic nature. She was a member of the Little Owls' Society, a ladies' group which met in each other's houses. The nine papers written by her include: *Are Modern Manners Improving?*; *Does the Influence of Women for Good or Evil Preponderate in Shakespeare?*; and *The Pre-Raphaelite Movement – its Aims and Works*. Even so, there was still time for her to oversee the household. Sir James employed ten indoor

Emily Kitson, my beautiful god-mother, in court dress aged about 27.

63

servants. The highest paid was Gorman, the butler, who received £60 a year and his own house. They had ten days' annual holiday. Female servants had to be home by 9.00pm on weekdays and 9.30pm on Saturdays. Their tasks were meticulously listed by Emily. Maids rose at 5.00am in order to clean the house before the guests were awake. It was now known that dirt and disease were linked, so fitted carpets, which might contain germs, were discarded and rugs that could be lifted, beaten and cleaned appeared instead upon highly polished floors.

When Sir James bought Gledhow, he employed the Leeds architects Chorley and Connor to enlarge John Carr's classic design. The original white stucco was now begrimed with industrial smoke. A three-storied wing was added to the north elevation to provide a billiard-room, a large sitting-room and more bedrooms. There were also two bathrooms – a welcome innovation at that time. The servants slept in the attics and their view of the park was restricted by a balustrade that encircled the house. This was a common device to protect the family from the gaze of their staff when they strolled in the garden. The simple lines of Carr's original design were now hidden beneath the flamboyant Victoriana which proclaimed to the world the power and largesse of the self-made man. Inside, little of Carr's work remained. Instead, the rooms were decorated with a pseudo-Jacobean carved dado together with a galaxy of highly coloured wallpapers. In the dining-room hung *Forget-me-not*, Sir John Millais' portrait of his daughter, which Sir James bought because she looked like Emily. Despite the destruction of much of Carr's earlier work, Gledhow was seen as symbolic of the solidity of Sir James's life. It was not a showpiece – it was a home.[81]

His 'fiery trial' did not fell this giant of a man. In 1895 he was elected as the Liberal MP for Colne Valley and the following year he was paid a signal honour by the Tory members of Leeds City Council, who nominated him as Mayor. His reaction was touching and typical. He told Herbert Gladstone: 'I have, saying I would never consent, consented. What a fellow, you will say. He will break down. He has too much on his hands already. He will and he has. ...

It seems to be a duty I can render to my native place and having in mind certain rebuffs and personal experiences of a distressing nature, it seems to be good of my fellow townsmen to propose this to me in a very handsome manner.'[82] He must have been much loved. The *Leeds Mercury* subsequently reported: 'We are happy to record the absolute and uncontrolled strength with which the new Mayor... rose to the dignity and importance of the great position to which he had been called.'[83]

Queen Victoria marked her Diamond Jubilee in 1897, and there was much entertaining to do – dinners to Her Majesty's judges; a great reception and ball in January; and a juvenile fancy dress party the next day, when Roland appeared as the duellist *Gil de Berault* and Olive as a shepherdess. On the morning of the Jubilee, it was announced that Her Majesty had been 'pleased to confer the title... of Lord Mayor' upon Sir James. In everything, Emily had been at his side. At the end of the year, he sat down to write to his daughter: 'The Lord Mayor desires to thank the Lady Mayoress for the assiduity, grace and dignity with which she has aided him in... the duties of his office.'[84]

In November 1898, Sir James visited the Baku oilfield on the Caspian Sea in which he had an interest.[85] He was accompanied by Herbert and Henry Gladstone, the politician sons of the former Prime Minister. Sir James wrote home regularly describing his travels. They travelled from Dover to Ostend and then spent two days in the train to St Petersburg – 'a pleasant journey and excellent food in the train restaurant'. Letters from the Gladstone family presented to the Russian customs 'caused our effects to be passed without examination'. After spending 58 hours in the train from Moscow, travelling at 20 mph, they arrived in Vladikafcas[86] on the Black Sea, a journey of 1,200 miles. Russian trains at that time were not laid on sleepers but directly on to the metalled or earth surface, and thus had to travel very slowly for fear of breaking up the tracks – 'the carriages are kept at a very high temperature, too high for Englishmen – water for lavatory purposes is rather scarce.' Crossing the Darriel Pass, north of Tiflis, they could see the snow-capped mountains of the Caucasus.[87] 'In all the post

Interior views of Gledhow Hall. From top left, Sir James Kitson's study *c* 1885 (the portrait may be of his mother); the dining-room *c* 1900 (with Millais' portrait of his daughter *Forget Me Not*); Emily Kitson's boudoir *c* 1900; and a bathroom *c* 1885 (with all the latest mod cons).

GLEDHOW HALL. LEEDS.
J. Kitson Esqre Baqer
BATH-ROOM IN BURMANTOFT FAIENCE.
Messrs Chorley and Connon
Architects

67

station stables, they keep a camel about the yard so that the horses may... not be startled by them when they meet... the bears were chained up as family pets. They are caught in the mountains. Tiflis is eastern, asiatic, with lots of quaint and savage looking Caucasians.' On 15 November they arrived in Baku. Sir James wrote to his son Edward: 'I wish I had brought you with us – it is such a wonderful experience... our first visit was to Bibi Eibat to see the works of the Russian Company. ...They were drilling wells and the process of lowering rods and drawing corks was very curious and effective. No.30 well was spouting continuously and the naptha was running away in a full continuous stream. They are expecting a fountain at one well before we leave. There were 13 boilers in a row, all fired by petroleum, only two men to look after them. ... We saw the plates pierced by the spout, cast iron plates 6 ins. thick, which looked like armour plates which had had shots through them. ... The people here have faith that the oil will last for years to come. ... The oil wells are covered with great wooden pyramidal houses in which are the boring and pumping apparatus. They are 50 and 60 feet high and... are crowded together and look, at a distance, like a forest.'[88]

Herbert Gladstone was also enjoying himself. He told Emily: 'Sir James is in wonderful form... the luncheon we had in the middle of the wells! It lasted a full hour. ... Sir James began with two glasses of vodka – went on to beer and coffee. ... I long for an English fire and detest the endless little dishes of caviar, sardines, sausages, smoked salmon, pickles and indescribable things which the Russians opened half an hour before they begin dinner.'[89]

They stayed at the Hôtel de l'Europe at Baku, a port on the Caspian Sea. Sir James wrote: 'The sitting room we have is good, but they have to come through my bedroom into it. There is one sitz bath which goes round. I get it first and [then] it is snatched away for Henry.' On 21 November, they went out to 'our Baku oil wells' in full evening dress at eight in the morning to meet Prince Galitzin, the Governor of the Caucasus. 'He came at 12 preceded by Cossacks and outriders. He stopped his carriage, descended and shook hands. ... Was very cordial. I had to do the talking

Sir James Kitson in his
ceremonial robes as first
Lord Mayor of Leeds, 1897.

being the linguist of the party. My French was very useful.'

The following day, the Prince, who was 'courteous and affable', delayed their departure. He spent an hour 'on our property at Baku Eibert. ... Just after he arrived, a fountain spouted. ... He was contented with our new works and showed it by inviting our party to go out with him to see the gas bubbling up in the sea, lighted and burning. They did fire the gas but it did not last long owing to the strong wind blowing.' [90]

To reach Batoum, a 'dull shipping port'[91] on the Black Sea, from Baku, they travelled west for two nights and one day: 'The Russian trains travel slowly, so barring the jolting and the total absence of sheets, the dearth of water and the irregularity of feeding, we got on very well in our compartments.' Their journey home took them via Constantinople, 'which is picturesque and strange, but nothing compensates for dirt and neglect'. At Budapest they were in

The drawing-room at Gledhow Hall in about 1890.

splendid quarters overlooking the Danube. 'By contrast with the places we have been in, this hotel is superb. I have had a luxurious bath in a white tiled room which I long to reproduce.' They had travelled 7,000 miles by land and sea.

For an engineer of Sir James's repute, the whole visit had been memorable. On his return home, life continued its normal pattern. He continued to serve his 'native place', and attended the House of Commons regularly; it was said that, had it not been for his deafness, he would have been in the Cabinet.[92] Two days before he died he wrote to Herbert Gladstone, 'I still feel I should have done better than I have done if I had not been so deaf.'[93] The condition was genetic and afflicted his son Albert, his daughters Emily and Hilda, and his granddaughter Emily (later known as Sylvia).

In 1905, the 23-year-old Roland was in some sort of trouble, the nature of which we do not know. On 31 July, his father wrote to his half-sister Emily: 'No, I have had no talk with Roland. I had with Olive, who is very sensible.' Two weeks later, there had been some sort of consultation with his son. He wrote again to Emily on 15 August: 'Roland has been talking to me and I have told him it is premature. He is, of course, in trouble – the first real trial he has had to face. He will have to go through the fire. We shall see if he will be constant under his mother's protests. I told him you knew, but don't write to him about it.' Was it some sort of money worry? Or a gambling debt? Was he in the grip of pressing creditors? Had he got a young woman into trouble? We do not know, nor do we know his mother's part in this, except that her former husband considered her a bad influence.

Portrait of Lord Airedale by John Singer Sargent, 1905.

Sir James Kitson and his daughter Emily and friends outside Gledhow Hall in about 1905. Sir James was an early enthusiast for motoring.

It was in this year that James was painted by John Singer Sargent, society's favourite portrait painter and much in demand. Apparently Sargent himself travelled north to paint this captain of industry, testimony to his sitter's status.[94] His subject is depicted in evening dress, with downward glance and an expression of both strength and melancholy.

Entertaining at Gledhow was on a brilliant scale, with no expense spared. Dinner parties, tennis parties, dances and balls followed in quick succession. The largest of the balls was on 11 January 1907, when 250 guests were invited; owing to a spate of influenza, only 170 turned up. Sixty people sat down to supper at one sitting, served by 18 waiters, and they drank six dozen bottles of champagne. Guests danced to the White Viennese band, who had been summoned from London. Emily, who supervised everything, has left five pages of description: 'Marquee built on the lawn by Mr Peck. ... The decorations were white with green smilax and ribbon bows with electric light underneath – this was arranged all round the sides of the room... a large space was left for sitting out

72

Sir James Kitson and Roland outside Gledhow Hall, c 1905.

and festoons and baskets of pink roses were arranged (Rose "Papa Goutier")... the room was heated by hot water pipes, connected with boiler in cellar, heated from the gas meter.' The cost was £301, 3 shillings and 6 pence, and was remembered by one guest when he was an old man: 'The bill for the marquee at Gledhow!! the dead leaves of a brilliant gathering. I can see Uncle James and Emily "receiving" in the exit from the hall to tent, the passage flanked by high screens of Gloire de Dijon roses. It was rumoured 2,000 from the South of France... silks, diamonds, hunting pink, chatter and laughter. ... BUT I was at Gledhow that night.'[95]

On 27 June 1907, Sir James Kitson was raised to the peerage as Baron Airedale of Gledhow, his title taken from the industrial valley in which his engineering works, bearing the same name, were placed. A few days later he wrote to Herbert Gladstone: 'I am thankful... that my... labour brought me into some contact with your noble father, the touch of his hand, the courtesies he gave me have sanctified my life. ... I think you have been the moving force in bringing the Prime Minister to offer me this new honour.'[96]

One letter of congratulation touched him greatly. It was from the far-off days at Wortley, when he would arrive on horseback to court Emily Cliff. The writer, in the deferential tone of those days, asked pardon for 'taking the liberty of writing to you.... I was the stable lad and... called..."Little Bob" but perhaps you have quite forgotten me .... You then taught me a lesson of punctuality and gentleness which I have tried to emulate ever since. It was your custom to come into the stable and say "Now Bob, bring my horse to the front door at ten" and punctual to the minute, the dear young lady who was the flower of the family and her lover came out... you never kept the stable boy waiting. Your kindness towards me then has caused me to have many feelings of affection towards yourself.'

By November 1907, James's health was causing concern and he was advised to 'slack off a bit'. Two months later, now a Privy Councillor, he was invited to move the Address to the Throne at the State Opening of Parliament, which set out Liberal Government policy for the coming session. His views on current issues reveal the measure of the man. His preparation was meticulous and he consulted Sir Edward Grey so that he made no mistake about foreign affairs. He told Emily: 'The mat of the hansom in which I returned just now from the Foreign Office was stamped E.K. so I thought that was lucky.'[97] Afterwards *The Times* reported that Lord Airedale had 'highly praised the recent tendencies of friendship with Germany. He warmly approved the arrangements with Russia and deplored the condition to which things had been reduced in Macedonia.'[98] On old age pensions he argued that 'some provision should be made for the distressed in their old age.' He said that the reduction of licensing hours would 'contribute materially to the elevation of the working people'[99], and considered that 'simple Bible teaching in the primary schools' is the only system that can hope to teach religious knowledge; he deplored 'merely secular teaching'.[100] As an industrialist, he was not in favour of the reduction of hours in the mines.[101]

The same evening he wrote to Emily from the Reform Club: 'I have made a 25 mins. speech in the Lords. In my P.C. uniform. The Prince of Wales was present... the House was full. Londonderry, Middleton, Avebury... congratulated me... Albert and Roland were there. Albert, as a Peer's eldest son, at the throne steps.'[102]

He spent Christmas 1908 at Gledhow without Emily, who had been unwell. Her father wrote to her at Bournemouth, where she was recuperating, describing the 'rope of pearls' which was his present to her: 'Dobson's man says it carries 250 large pearls and the same amount... of small ones. Some day, when you weary of reading, you might count them.' He added that he thought Edward was 'strangely unwise in the management of his health'.[103]

Cars were beginning to take over from the ubiquitous horse. In October 1910 Sir James observed to Emily: 'The motor conveyance is a great advantage. It was quite striking to see the number of motors. Horse conveyances will soon be cleared clean away.' Emily's health continued to be poor, and in the autumn of 1910 she had a major operation in London. She missed the last four Christmases of her father's life at Gledhow and spent much of her time convalescing in either Bournemouth or Madeira. On 25 December that year, the family were joined by Emily and Doris, Albert's eldest and third daughters.[104] Although they were 19 and 16 respectively, they were 'most alarmed' at the thought of the dinner party. Doris's aunt Hilda recalled that Doris sat next to Arthur Swayne who was 'very good at making conversation with the child. Little Emily looks so pretty this year, her complexion is most brilliant and her figure quite good now; she has not much conversation of course.'[105]

On 18 March, James attended a great dinner at the Reform Club to honour the appointment of his old friend, Herbert Gladstone, as the first Governor-General of South Africa. An idea of the gargantuan appetites of the day can be obtained from the menu:

MENU

Caviar sur Glace
Et
Sardines Americaines
* * *
Royale Tortue claire[106]
* * *
Filets de Sole à la Botha
* * *
Truite froide à la Norvegienne
* * *
Terrine de Cailles à la Gladstone[107]
* * *
Cotelette de Pré-Salé à la Reforme[108]
Pommes Nouvelles
* * *
Petit Poussin à la Broche
Salade de laitue
* * *
Haricots Verts à la Française
* * *
Poirs glacée a l'Edouard VII
Petits fours
* * *
Croute à l'Unite
* * *
Dessert et Café Noir

Sherry: Butler's Pale   *Liqueurs*
Hock: Steinberger 1900   *Cigars:* Flor de Cuba Rothschild 1908
Champagne: Krug, Private Cuvée, 1900   La Corona Corona 1908
Claret: Château Laujac 1878
Port: Cockburn's 1872   *Egyptian cigarettes*

The same evening, although he must have been tired, he did not fail to tell Emily of the occasion: 'Herbert made an excellent speech .... Lord Crewe was remarkably good .... I shall never say he is dull again. He made a nice reference to his noble friend Lord Airedale under whose roof he met Herbert in years gone by, when I was known as "young Kitson".'

Two months later, on 6 May 1910, Edward VII died and the country prepared for a new monarch. At the end of the year, when preparations for the crowning of George V were well under way, James roguishly told Emily: 'I have given notice to the Earl Marshal, the Coronation is not to proceed without my presence'.[109] Sadly, three months later, he died in France and it was his son, Albert Ernest, who attended the ceremony in his place.

By the early twentieth century, James Kitson was a very rich man indeed. (At his death, he left over one million pounds – a huge sum in 1911.)[110] He spent lavishly and travelled widely, staying only in the best hotels. The Meurice in Paris, where he died, was one of his favourites. Emily, who had acquired her father's expensive tastes, was hugely indulged. On 1 January 1911 he told her of a visit he had made to his bank: 'I told the Manager that I required £80,000 .... He said "certainly". ... I didn't tell him that it was required for the hotel bills I was incurring in various parts of England.'[111]

Lord Airedale and Emily Kitson in the south of France 1911, shortly before his death.

In February 1911, James and Emily left for their usual spring holiday in the south of France, where they were joined by Roland and Olive. James seemed well and in good spirits.

On his last day in Menton, after 'a very happy three weeks', he wrote to Herbert Gladstone, now a Viscount. He told him how he had visited his notorious sister-in-law, Mrs Arthur Kitson, now ensconsed in a handsome villa she had built on Cap Ferrat.[112] The 'avenues of cypress trees' reminded him how he 'would like such a home for my declining years'. He would now go home to 'my direction of industries, of Banks and Railways with my average ability and shall work to the end ... giving way to sons, each time they display any desire ... to take up anything I am guiding'. His deafness had been a constant barrier, as it was to his eldest son.

The following night, 16 March, returning home in the train from Beaulieu to Paris, he had a heart attack. Despite the attentions of a Danish doctor on the train, and the care of an English doctor at the Meurice, he died at the hotel with three of his children at his side. There was much grief in his native city. Newspapers described the passing of 'the foremost citizen of Leeds'. The flag on the Town Hall flew at half-mast for a week. On 22 March, the funeral procession of this 'merchant prince' wound its way from City Square and Mill Hill Chapel to Roundhay churchyard, where he was buried beside his parents, his wife and his two brothers. Leeds had never seen anything like it.

For Emily it was a devastating blow. Few fathers and daughters were so close. He had been her life, and for him she had given up hopes of a brilliant marriage. In 1909 he had rented a large, imposing house in London, number 3 Cadogan Square. I remember it well. This was always intended to be 'Emily's house', but her father's sudden death intervened. Surprisingly, he had made no mention in his will. It was her brother, Albert, who, with 'characteristic generosity'[113] leased for her 23 Upper Grosvenor Street. Emily was not an easy person and had been hugely spoiled. She tried to forget her family's humble origins. She was apparently incensed by E.K.Clark's *The Kitsons of Leeds*, which referred to her grandfather as the son of a publican.[114] At the time of his death she was only 45 but still spurned offers of marriage.[115]

So ended the life of this giant of a man. He had lived at the hub of the great world and was much loved. He overcame the double tragedy of the death of his first wife and his desertion by his second. 'Never look back' was his mantra. Of his four sons, only one inherited his genius. Albert's inability to breed an heir must have caused him anguish, but in Roland, the child of his errant wife, he had a son who would maintain the lustre of the Kitson name.

It is a sadness to me that my great-grandfather, considered to be 'the greatest of the English iron masters' and 'one of the most influential men in Britain... a driving force in the evolution of the

Industrial Revolution',[116] should have been so undervalued by his own family. My mother never mentioned his name and I doubt whether she, or her sisters, had any idea of his worth.

This memoir is my tribute.

Notes

[1] Now demolished. It lay at the western edge of Woodhouse Carr.

[2] Born 1786.

[3] Born 1784.

[4] James was the oldest of six children, the others being: Anthony, born at 8.30pm on 19 January 1810, registered at the Methodist Chapel, Leeds; William, born at 6.15pm on 7 April 1813; John, born at 5.15am on 18 February (y.n.k.); Martha, born at 7.30pm on 15 February 1819; Hannah, born at 8.00am on 24 August 1823 and registered at the Albion Chapel. The births of all the children except Anthony and Hannah were registered at the Old Church, Leeds. Information from family Bible, courtesy of Anthea Boylston.

[5] G.Talbot Griffith, *James Kitson and Some Others*, unpublished ms, 1970 p.3. Courtesy of West Yorkshire Archives. WYL 844/44.

[6] E. Kitson Clark, *Kitsons of Leeds*, Locomotive Publishing, London, 1938, p.3.

[7] E. Kitson Clark, *Kitsons of Leeds*, p.5.

[8] See Appendix 2 for the *Oxford Dictionary of National Biography*'s article on James Kitson. (Both were born in 1807.)

[9] Born in 1806, Ann was the second child of John Newton and Ann Kay of Bedale (1778–1862). The latter's brother (Fretwell) owned the Talbot Estate in Briggate, Leeds. He left a large amount of money to the Newton family which resulted in a long law suit to the detriment of the Newtons – shades of Jarndyce v Jarndyce in *Bleak House*. Hilda Kitson to E.F. Clark, 1936.

[10] The family trees, planned for Vol. 2, will show this extended family.

[11] He would already have known the first working steam railway in the world, the Middleton Railway, a private line about 3 miles long from Middleton colliery through Hunslet to a staithe on the river Aire. It was commissioned in 1812, and four locomotives did the work of 50 horses. Information from E.F. Clark.

[12] Todd's wife's niece was probably Ann Newton – hence the connection. Information from E.F. Clark.

[13] Robert, son of the well-known George, was largely responsible for building the famous *Rocket*.

[14] This was *Lion*, which in 1937 appeared in the film *Victoria the Great,* starring Anna Neagle, and, even more famously, in *The Titfield Thunderbolt,* an Ealing comedy of 1952. She is now the second oldest working locomotive in the world and will shortly find a permanent home in Liverpool. Information from E.F. Clark.

[15] Kitson & Co. occupied Airedale Foundry until 1945 when it was sold to a

local engineering company. The buildings have since been demolished. Kitson's ceased to build locomotives in 1938. Information from E.F.Clark.

[16] E. Kitson Clark, *Kitsons of Leeds*.

[17] Some Kitson engines can be seen today at the following locations:
South Devon Railway, Buckfastleigh
Historic Dockyard, Chatham
North Yorkshire Moors Railway, Grosmont
Llangollen Railway, Denbighshire
Northamptonshire Ironstone Railway Trust, Hunsbury
N.Tyneside Steam Railway, West Chirton
The 'Aerolite' an engine which was the twin of a medal-winning locomotive built by Kitsons for the Great Exhibition of 1851 was bought by the North Eastern Railway. www.steamlocomotive.info

[18] My father worked there after his marriage to my mother. He was unqualified for anything else.

[19] Unitarians believed in One God and not the Trinity. As Non-Conformists or Dissenters, they were considered socially inferior by some Anglicans and their way of life was severely restricted. See F.L. Cross (ed.), *The Oxford Book of the Christian Church*, OUP, Oxford, 1957.

[20] G.Talbot Griffith, *James Kitson and Some Others*, p.18.

[21] Janet Wicksteed, daughter of the Mill Hill Minister. G.Talbot Griffith, *James Kitson and Some Others*, p.12.

[22] Though parts have been demolished, Elmet Hall still stands, much of it altered. The Army requisitioned the house during the Second World War, and later it became a school for autistic children. It is now offices.

[23] Steven Burt, *History of Roundhay Park*, published by Steven Burt, Leeds LS16 8LL. www.forp.co.uk

[24] James Kitson to Herbert Gladstone, 8 July 1885. G.Talbot Griffith, *James Kitson and Some Others*.

[25] See page 49 for details of the scandal.

[26] Notes by Brian Matthews, p.2 (see page 49). See also Appendix 3 for the the *Oxford Dictionary of National Biography*'s article on James Kitson.

[27] 1829–1928, sister of Grosvenor Talbot, close friend of Fred's brother James.

[28] Henry Herbert's grandson, Timothy, achieved distinction as a politician, serving as Conservative MP for Richmond, North Yorkshire, from 1959 to 1983; he was a Parliamentary Private Secretary to Edward Heath when Heath was Prime Minister, and was knighted in 1974.

[29] Born in 1843 and presumably called after Robert Hawthorn (1796–1867), a well-known Newcastle locomotive builder.

[30] His brother James had already bought Gledhow (see below). Perhaps John Hawthorn inherited Elmet because his two older brothers received the foundry.

[31] Sir James Kitson to his daughter Emily, 1899, G.Talbot Griffith, *James Kitson and Some Others*, p.17.

[32] G.Talbot Griffith, *James Kitson and Some Others*, p.16.

33 Fragment of autobiography left by Beatrice. Courtesy of Anthea Boylston.

34 The Leslie Lohman Gay Foundation. www.leslielohman.org/WvonGloeden

35 Daphne Phelps, *A House in Sicily*, Virago, London, 1999.

36 The Leslie Lohman Gay Foundation. www.leslielohman.org/WvonGloeden.

37 Many are in the care of the Brotherton Library, Leeds University (bequest of Daphne Phelps).

38 G.Talbot Griffith, *James Kitson and Some Others*, p.17.

39 Women were not awarded full degrees until after the Second World War.

40 Ethel Mallinson's paintings still fetch good prices at auction today.

41 Hilda Kitson to her sister Emily, 31 January 1895.

42 He left 600 of these to Leeds City Art Gallery. Sadly, although they were given as a permanent bequest for the citizens of Leeds, they are not on public view (June 2006) as there is no curator to show them. Some can be seen in Norwich Castle Museum & Art Gallery.

43 As remembered by her nephew, Brian Matthews.

44 Arthur was a gifted engineer and designer of the powerful pressure lighthouse oil lanterns used by Trinity House. One can be seen at the Trinity House museum in Penzance. Information from E.F.Clark.

45 *Oxford Dictionary of National Biography*, article on William Playfair. It was later reduced, on appeal, to £9,200 (about £600,000 today).

46 By E. Kitson Clark. Information from E.F.Clark.

47 Grosvenor Talbot married Clara, the sister of Emily Cliff. He was thus James' brother-in-law twice over because his sister Ellen married Frederick William. G.Talbot Griffith (author of the memoir) was their grandson.

48 His largesse, in the form of the Cliff Trust, has come down to my generation. The Trust was set up by Walter Cliff (Emily's brother), who died a bachelor in 1917. It was left to the many descendents of Joseph Cliff (his father) and was wound up in 1997 on the death of the last main beneficiary.

49 Alice Dewhurst (1819–1892).

50 Remembered by Janet Wicksteed, daughter of Charles, the Mill Hill Minister. G.Talbot Griffith, *James Kitson and Some Others*, p.13.

51 Founders of St Hilda's College, Oxford, and North London Collegiate School respectively.

52 In West Yorkshire Archives. WRA 893/22.

53 Now in West Yorkshire Archives. WRA 893/22. It is very difficult to read.

54 G.Talbot Griffith, *James Kitson and Some Others*, p.40.

55 G.Talbot Griffith, *James Kitson and Some Others*, p.37.

56 William Cliff (her brother) to Emily (his niece) on James's death, 22 March 1911. G.Talbot Griffith, *James Kitson and Some Others*, p.41.

57 James Kitson to Herbert Gladstone. G.Talbot Griffith, *James Kitson and Some Others*, p.97.

58 G.Talbot Griffith, *James Kitson and Some Others*, p.98.

59 A watercolour by J.M.W. Turner painted in 1816 showed Gledhow from the hillside across the valley, with a lake in the foreground and the house, in those days, the colour of yellow sandstone. It was left to Emily, who bequeathed it

to Evelyn's son, Guy, because one of his names was Kitson. When she died in 1962, it was sold, to the fury of some of the family, to cover Death Duties. He received £4000 in lieu. (Information from Guy Kitson Nevett.)

[60] James Kitson to Emily 1 June 1885. G. Talbot Griffith, *James Kitson and Some Others*, p.99.

[61] Mary Laura Kitson to Herbert Gladstone, February 1886.

[62] West Yorkshire Archives. WYL 893/22.

[63] Francis Roberts, my second cousin, remembers a rumour to this effect.

[64] On 2 March 1887.

[65] West Yorkshire Archives. WYL 893/22.

[66] Reproduced on page 57.

[67] Gladstone was then Leader of the Opposition, following the defeat of his third administration over Home Rule for Ireland.

[68] *The Times*, 13 April 1923.

[69] Information from Francis Roberts and Anthea Boylston.

[70] G. Talbot Griffith, *James Kitson and Some Others*, p.106.

[71] Although she was left a smaller sum than her half-sisters in her putative father's will, she and her brother Roland had apparently benefited from an earlier settlement dated 1881 at the time of their father's second marriage.

[72] Anecdote from Violet Shiell.

[73] Louisa Griffith to Talbot Griffith, G. Talbot Griffith, *James Kitson and Some Others*, p.109.

[74] Last Will & Testament of James Kitson, lst Lord Airedale, 13 August 1909. The three other sons, Albert, Edward and Roland were each left £100,000 about £7 million at today's values.

[75] Now in Leeds Record Office: Susan Lasdun, *The Victorians at Home*, Weidenfeld and Nicolson, London, 1981, p.140.

[76] In 1880 he became MP for West Leeds when his father won the Midlothian seat.

[77] W.E. Gladstone was Prime Minister from 1868 to 1874, in 1886 and from 1892 to 1894.

[78] Charles Dickens, *Great Expectations*.

[79] This had been lent to Violet Shiell for Cynthia's wedding in 1946 through the good offices of Emily's sister, Hilda. Hilda also possessed a veil which she lent to Enid for her wedding in 1924.

[80] Anecdote from my mother.

[81] Susan Lasdun, *The Victorians at Home*.

[82] JK to Herbert Gladstone, 25 October 1896. G. Talbot Griffith, *James Kitson and Some Others*, p.149.

[83] *Leeds Mercury*, Nov. 1896. G. Talbot Griffith, *James Kitson and Some Others*, p.149.

[84] Sir James was Leeds' first Lord Mayor. Forty-five years later, in 1942, his niece, Beatrice Kitson, became the first female Lord Mayor, with Elinor Lupton as her Lady Mayoress.

[85] Sir James later became Chairman of the Baku Russian Oil Company.

[86] Now Ordzhonikidze.

[87] The main mountain is Kasbec, which is higher than Mont Blanc.

[88] Sir James Kitson to Edward Kitson, 15 November 1898. G.Talbot Griffith, *James Kitson and Some Others*, p.160.

[89] Herbert Gladstone to Emily Kitson, 17 November 1898.

[90] G.Talbot Griffith, *James Kitson and Some Others*, p.163.

[91] Now Batumi.

[92] Obituary March 1911. G.Talbot Griffith, *James Kitson and Some Others*, p.112.

[93] Lord Airedale to Viscount Gladstone, 14 March 1911. G.Talbot Griffith, *James Kitson and Some Others*, p. 249.

[94] See page 71. www.leicestergalleries.com

[95] Frank Talbot to Talbot Griffith, *c.* 1960.

[96] James Kitson to Herbert Gladstone, 7 July 1907. Sir Henry Campbell-Bannerman was the Prime Minister.

[97] 28 January 1908. G.Talbot Griffith, *James Kitson and Some Others*, p.169.

[98] *The Times*, 30 January 1908.

[99] Victorian licensing hours were long and demanding: eighteen hours a day, 4am to 10pm, seven days a week, closed only during Divine Service, Christmas Day and Good Friday. This was ideal for shift workers.

[100] It will be remembered that both he and Emily Cliff were Sunday School teachers.

[101] The Coal Mines Regulation Act 1908, generally known as the 'Eight Hours Act', limited the hours miners spent underground to seven and a half.

[102] James Kitson to Emily, 29 January 1908. G.Talbot Griffith, *James Kitson and Some Others*, p.171.

[103] Edward died on 15 January 1922 aged 48. The cause of death was given as 'heart failure following gastro-enteritis induced by habitual use of paraldehyde', a sedative given for epileptic seizures (and occasionally to treat alcohol withdrawal).

[104] Marguerite Emily later changed her name to Sylvia. 'Doris' was my mother.

[105] Poor little Emily, already deaf. G.Talbot Griffith, *James Kitson and Some Others*.

[106] Turtle soup.

[107] Terrine of quail.

[108] Lamb cutlet.

[109] 22 December 1910. West Yorkshire Archives. WYL 893/22

[110] The equivalent of about £75 million today.

[111] West Yorkshire Archives. WYL 893/22. About £5 million today.

[112] Presumably with the fat proceeds of the libel case.

[113] G.Talbot Griffith, *James Kitson and Some Others*, p.114.

[114] Information from Violet Shiell.

[115] G.Talbot Griffith, *James Kitson and Some Others*, p.257.

[116] See his portrait by John Singer Sargent at www.leicestergalleries.com

Coats of arms of the McNaughtons (top), the Schunck family (bottom left) and Baron Airedale (bottom right).

Chapter 3

Parents and Grandparents 1892–1933

'Tell me this: who begot thee?
Marry, the son of my grandfather'

The Two Gentlemen of Verona 3.1.287

My parents, John McNaughton and Doris Claire Kitson, should never have married. This ill-matched pair met through mutual friends during the Great War, on a Scottish grouse moor.

My father was the elder of two sons of the Reverend George Ferrier Anderson McNaughton, a devout, impoverished and much-loved minister of the Church of Scotland.[1] My grandfather came from one of those intellectual Scottish families where wit and erudition were more important than money.[2] His mother, Ellen Ferrier, came from a long line of writers, artists, booksellers and publishers.[3] (My mother, who had received a paltry education, was totally at sea when staying with Jack and his cousins, because the entire conversation at mealtimes was conducted in quotations.[4]) He had an older brother, James John,[5] and a younger, David Norman,[6] who married Christina Leck (Aunt Teenie) and a sister, Euphans.[7]

After graduating in divinity from Glasgow University, George McNaughton married his bride, Margaret Anderson,[8] at Pollockshields Established Church on 7 April 1891, her 29th birthday. He was 35 years old and a curate at Glasgow Cathedral, and had delayed his marriage until he could be sure of obtaining a living. (The heavily engraved silver tray, presented to him by the congregation, was stolen in the Reedham burglary of 1980. We used to keep the drinks on it – which would have pleased my father.) The following year, he was offered the living of Carsphairn, Galloway, where his two sons, my father, Jack,[9] and his younger brother, Stewart, were

My grandmother Margaret Anderson (later Margaret McNaughton) aged about nine.

born.[10] For more than 20 years, he had to be content with being merely an 'assistant' to the absentee Mr Finlay. It was not until 6 August 1913 that he was admitted to the 'full charge', an event that was marked by a handsome silver-cornered blotter. It must have been a great sadness that neither his beloved wife nor his older son were present.

The boys spent a happy but Calvinistic childhood in Galloway. The Sabbath in the grey stone Manse was gloomy, dour and solemn. The boys were expected to attend kirk at least three times, and to read only improving books – a typical Victorian childhood, in fact, and one that put Jack off church for ever. Their great friend, and conspirator in their childish games, was Bessie, the cook, who made them delicious girdle scones and their favourite pudding, Floating Island, blobs of egg white floating in a sea of strawberry jam.[11] Jack was a boy who loved the open air and who found no greater happiness than to roam the moors near his home with gun or rod. He was also a reader, and his passion was Rudyard Kipling. The brothers were very different, the younger idolising the older, which was to have lasting consequences. The fates had not treated them equally. Jack was fair and handsome, and the gift of 'charm' would ease his passage through life. His brother was bespectacled and studious. Their characters were different as well. Jack's mind was lightweight, and he was devoid

My great-great-uncle Francis Finlayson who found W. Niven's story.

86

My aunt and godmother
Kate Anderson (later Kate
Gray) aged about 17.

of humour. Stewart was serious and intent, but possessed a dry
wit. After Cargilfield, a renowned Scottish preparatory school, the
boys in due course went on to Fettes. Jack had an uneventful, if un-
academic, career there, while Stewart's claim to fame was as the
only boy who has ever been prayed for in Chapel for being consti-
pated for three weeks. (Jack handed down the McNaughton cast-
iron digestion to his elder daughter.)

When he was 14, Jack suffered the first sorrow of his young life.
His mother, Margaret, beautiful, intelligent and talented and a
gifted pianist and linguist, had suffered for some time from rheumatic arthritis. Now she fell ill with breast cancer. Her marriage
had been supremely happy and when she died, on 6 June 1906,
aged only 44, Jack was heartbroken. He treasured her last letter to
him, written in pencil in the garden a few days before her death,
telling him how much she loved him and asking him to look after
Stewart. He kept it all his life.[12]

The impact of this blow on George McNaughton can only be

My father Jack
McNaughton,
aged about four.

imagined, and irritation with his feckless older son, who appeared
to have no talents except his undoubted charm, began to show.
(There were distinct parallels with the next monarch and his
heir.[13]) When he left school at 18, Jack had no idea what to do.
Apart from his love of literature, and his skill with rod, gun and
horse, he had few assets that would earn him a living. There was no
family money, no great estate to fall back upon, and his father was
deeply concerned.

In the event he was sent down to London and enlisted with a
crammer to work for an exam.[14] He lodged at 4 Grenville Place
with Uncle Norman and his family, but had no great hope of success. On 18 October 1910 he told his father, 'I won't here [*sic*] for
a day or two yet how I have got on in the Qualifying but I am working up for the Competitive even if I have failed I won't have to

My grandmother
with my father Jack
as a baby, *c* 1892.

change my work at all for the next Competitive in June as the
periods in History and the Military Biography are the same.' As
always, his finances were strained. 'What am I to do about money
when I finish what I have got?' A few days later, his fears were realised. 'As you will know by this time, I *have* failed in that Exam. and
the result is that I don't know what to do.'

Whether it was Jack's idea or his father's I do not know, but for
whatever reason in 1912 he sailed for Canada, to Montreal. Here
his unbounded social gifts, his looks and charisma came into their

Jack as a Fettesian aged about 13.

own. Suddenly, having escaped the constant reproofs of his father, he found that he was a favourite – particularly with women. He felt little need to 'settle down' when life could be such fun, and he made no great effort to find a job. He acquired the lifestyle of a playboy, and party-going and girls became his main interests. (There are impassioned letters from his father urging him to take a grip upon himself, to earn some money and to stop wasting it on horses, cards and the fillies.) On 21 April 1912 he wrote to his father from Montreal. 'Wasn't that an awful accident that happened to the "Titanic"? ... Quite a lot of prominent Montrealers went down with her and it struck the city very hard ... because nearly everybody knows all the victims personally.'

The outbreak of war in August 1914 brought this idyllic lifestyle to an end, and in a way proved to be Jack's salvation. Far from home, he had but one thought, to join up. He immediately enlisted in the 42nd battalion of the Royal Highlanders of Canada – the Black Watch, his home regiment. He spent three years in the trenches of Flanders, where he was both wounded and gassed. (The gas left an enduring legacy in his lungs, which eventually killed him of emphysema at the age of 67.) I never remember him mentioning the war – anyone who has seen R.C. Sherriff's play *Journey's End* will understand why. His courage in leading a daring raid on enemy positions earned him the Military Cross.[15]

Captain John
McNaughton M.C.,
aged about 24.

Meanwhile Stewart, whose more serious character gained him his father's approval, enlisted as a Private in the Royal Army Medical Corps in the 52nd Lowland Division of the Mediterranean Expeditionary Force. In June 1915 he and his close friend, Randall Mill, sailed from Devonport for Egypt.[16] Despite the scorpions, lice and fleas of the Sahara, they wrote cheerful letters home.[17] 'The chief features of the place are flies, dust and wind, to

Private Stewart McNaughton, Jack's brother, who served as a nursing orderly during the First World War.

compensate for this we get wonderfully good food.... Most of the days – every day in fact – we dig. We dig ourselves into dug-outs – no... easy task in a soil as dry as the Sahara and as hard in parts as Edinburgh Castle rock... it is eleven weeks now since we felt a drop of rain.'[18] Reading, chess and bridge filled Stewart's leisure hours. 'I have been reading the *Golden Treasury*... as there's nothing else to read and have finished learning Arnold's "Rugby Chapel".'

92

It must have been agony for his widowed father to have his two sons in action. Stewart, at least, as a nursing orderly, was in a non-combative role. Although the glamorous Jack, a staff officer in France, was often in danger, he managed, according to Stewart, 'to dine in the best restaurants and patronise the buffets of charming Society Ladies'[19] – a custom he would continue throughout his life. Both boys were succoured by regular parcels of food and books from their family, particularly Aunt Kate and Uncle Willie.

Apparently Stewart was a competent medical orderly and his duties included 'giving a dose of Castor oil for almost any complaint... partly a precaution against malingering'. In September 1915, when in Gallipoli, he received an offer from their family doctor, Dr Ford, to return home as his assistant. Declining, with gratitude, Stewart added 'I don't want to leave the Corps on the Peninsular.'[20] The next day he wrote to his father, 'This is an interval between digging, we are just about finished with the dug-outs. ... I understand we will have another Hospital to dig when we have finished them.'

At last the rain arrived. 'It came on to rain about 4 a.m. and rained for about two hours... and reduced the place to a quagmire in about half an hour – about six inches in mud. We tried to protect ourselves... by putting our waterproofs on top of us, but we found we were lying in a puddle of mud in a short time.'

In December, Randall and Stewart 'had a hot tub... it was exactly six months... since we had our last hot bath in Dunfermline. You can imagine what a delight it was... for it is about a month since I had my last bathe and since then I've only been able to get the amount of washing that can be got out of a dixie[21] and that's precious little. The hot bath was absolutely ripping. A clean pailful of hot water and a tub in which you could sit down (I was lucky).[22] I believe we will get one now about every ten days or fourteen, so that's not so bad.'[23]

The following year, having been sent home on sick leave to recover from the gas, Jack accepted an invitation from his friend and neighbour Tom Wilson,[24] a subaltern in the Argylls, to shoot at nearby Moniaive.[25] Tom's sister Jane, and her schoolfriends

My mother
Doris Kitson,
aged about 16.

Evelyn and Doris Kitson, were part of the house party. (Although chronically short of money, because it never remained long in his pocket, Jack nevertheless acquired well-heeled and influential friends, who found his charm irresistible.) It was thus that Jack first set eyes on my mother, Doris. At 22, she was small, dark and brimming with life. She was also intelligent and highly sexed. After a sheltered childhood, in which she was brought up mainly by servants, she was relishing the freedom of country house parties where she found, somewhat to her surprise, that she was extremely attractive to men. The sight of this fair young man, in his Highland uniform and riding breeches, was a *coup de foudre*.

* * *

The second Baron Airedale, Albert Ernest, my grandfather, did not inherit the acumen of his father.[26] This small boy had lost his mother (three days before his tenth birthday) and by an ill-chance, at almost the same time, caught measles at Rugby which exacerbated his genetic ear trouble and left him profoundly deaf. There was, however, one good fairy at his christening, who gave him the gift of music, and this was to be his lifetime's solace. Despite his deafness, he became a talented pianist, probably to concert standard, and later sponsored many struggling young men, among them the virtuoso Solomon. Albert cannot have

Lord and Lady Airedale at the coronation of King George V, 1911.

My great-grand-
father Edward,
Baron von Schunck
(1816–99).

been unintelligent, for after Rugby, he went to Trinity College,
Cambridge. In stature, he was under-sized, and in Florence
Schunck made a predictable choice of wife, choosing the daughter
of a neighbouring family who were fellow-Unitarians.

I had always understood that the name Schunck was German. I
had hoped to find some mention of Florence's father Edward, my
great-grandfather, in the Yorkshire newspapers, for they were an

The suave Clifford
Kitson and his elder
brother Albert
Ernest, later 2nd
Baron Airedale and
my grandfather.

eminent family, but there was none. However, a family history
written by his son, also Edward, told me more.[27] (During the Great
War, the Schuncks, like the royal Saxe-Coburg-Gothas, felt com-
pelled to hide their Germanic origins, and assumed the name
Darnton.) From this I learned that the family could be traced back
to the 14th century, and that they were originally from the Span-
ish Netherlands, where, in 1719 they were raised to the rank of

My great-grand-
mother Kate
Schunck (Lupton)
with John Edward
Schunck, c 1873.

Baron with the right to call themselves 'von'. However, being
Lutherans, they were driven out in the religious persecutions by
successive Holy Roman Emperors. They fled to Hesse, where one
branch settled in Frankfurt and another in Hanau. In the early
19th century, now successful merchants and entrepreneurs, they
decided to try their luck in England. One of them, Edward (a first
cousin of my great-grandfather), settled in Manchester, where his
genius as a chemist earned him both fame and a great deal of
money.[28] [29] His cousin settled in Yorkshire, living the life of a well-

98

My great-great-grandfather
Darnton Lupton, Mayor of Leeds,
aged about 38.

heeled country gentleman. His house was also near the village of
Gledhow, and it was here that he met my great-grandmother,
Kate,[30] the only child of Darnton Lupton,[31] and married her in
1867. Their first child, Florence, married my grandfather, Albert
Ernest Kitson, in 1890.

They were an ill-matched pair. My grandfather, small and deaf,
and his half-German wife had seven children. They were all girls.
As each one arrived, there was dismay that the longed-for son, the
next Baron, had failed to materialise. On 28 July 1894, Albert
wrote from Gledhow Wood[32] to his sister, Emily: 'Another girl was
born at 12.25 last night .... I am so sorry it is not a boy – I am sure
we shall never have one. Three girls are quite enough, I think. The
new stranger is very strong and healthy – quite the biggest of the
lot.'[33] The new arrival was my mother, Doris.

Doris would inherit the sharp mind of her Kitson grandfather,
the only one of the seven to do so. Apart from Evelyn, who was my
mother's favourite, and Angela, most of the rest were lacking in
humour. Their names recalled the nurserymaids and under-
servants with whom they spent most of their time – Sylvia,[34]
Evelyn, Doris, Enid, Violet, Thelma, Angela. The children seldom

My grandmother
Florence Schunck
(later Florence
Kitson); this may
have been a be-
trothal photograph.

saw their parents, who were away much of the time. Many holidays
were spent at Cober Hill, Cloughton, near Scarborough, the
Victorian house which Albert Ernest had bought in 1891. The
nannies and servants held sway there and practised whatever
cruelties they liked. My mother recalled being locked in cupboards
for hours as a punishment. Perhaps as a result, she also suffered
from enuresis, a psychological malady quite misunderstood in
those days. One day she and her sister were promised a trip to

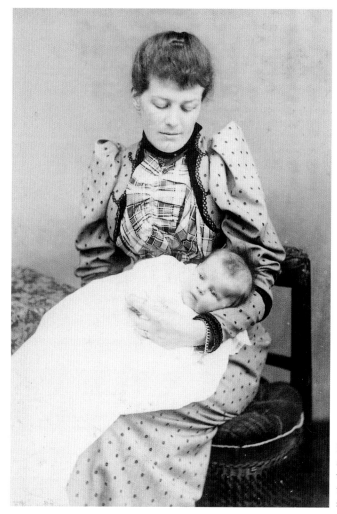

Florence Kitson
aged about 30
with baby Enid,
the fourth of her
seven daughters.

Scarborough to see the circus, but a spate of bed-wetting put this treat in jeopardy. 'If you wet your bed tonight, no circus tomorrow.' Of course the inevitable happened, and the treat was off. As she said, years later, 'would I have done it on purpose?'

My mother, rightly considered bright, was sent to Roedean preparatory school, which she loved. She should have gone on to the main school, where her intelligence would have been trained, but her sister Evelyn had been sent to Highfield, the fashionable

London school in Hendon. She nagged and nagged and eventually wore down her long-suffering mother. (Presumably her father took no interest in girls.)[35] So she joined Evelyn and learned nothing. Afterwards she said it was a big mistake. But she did meet some 'nice girls' like Jane Wilson, the daughter of Sir John Wilson, Bart, of Moniaive, which eventually led to the grouse moors and matrimony. When she left Highfield, she went to Paris to be 'finished'. Here, she rode side-saddle in the Bois de Boulogne on a black mare named Gilda.

In 1912, at the age of 17, she was presented at Court, and five years later she met my father on the grouse moors of Galloway. My father, always known as Jack, was tall, fair and handsome, a Captain in the Black Watch (42nd Royal Highlanders of Canada) and ADC to General McDonnell. It was 1916, and he was on leave from France, where a short time later he won the Military Cross for gallantry in a daring raid on enemy trenches in the Somme.[36] It was thus that he met my mother, a naive 22-year-old, who was immediately swept off her feet by this 'Young Lochinvar',[37] as she always called him.

In August 1916, under the blazing Egyptian sun, Stewart McNaughton was amazed to hear that his elder brother and Doris were engaged to be married. 'By Jove, young man', he wrote to Jack, 'you don't lack for nerve, nor do you waste your time.'[38] There was much excitement in Carsphairn, the McNaughton family home – Doris's title of 'The Hon.', as the daughter of a peer, added glamour. Their father was 'captivated ' and 'at the Lady's feet'.

The courtship was brief: a few rushed leaves from the Front, a few hurried dinners in London, an evening or two dancing at the Savoy where my grandfather kept a suite. The feelings of the young Scot, brought up frugally in the grey stone manse where every penny had to be counted, when he entered the gilded world of the second Baron Airedale can only be imagined. Albert had inherited from his father the large redbrick house in Cadogan Square, which had its own garden. When Jack arrived at the iron-grilled front door, to escort 'Miss Doris' for the evening, it was opened by Hemsley, the butler, behind whom stood a footman in yellow and

My mother Doris Kitson as an 18-year-old debutante in 1912.

navy blue livery. Although he may have found his prospective parents-in-law a little stiff, their delight in such an eligible and attractive young man, who was the first suitor of their daughters, was not surprising. There were, after all, six more. From Jack's viewpoint, his future appeared rosy. The end of the war was in sight, and with a rich father-in-law only too thankful to get the first of his brood off his hands Jack could see a life of idleness and luxury ahead. He lost no time in proposing to his 'wee thing', as he called his bride, who adored him, and the wedding day was fixed for 4 April 1918.

Alas, a week beforehand, the Germans decided to advance, and all leave was cancelled. Doris was distraught. Weeping, she sobbed that she knew he would be killed. On the evening of 3 April, she was being comforted by Mary, her old nanny, in the housekeeper's sitting room, when there was a knock on the door. Outside stood Jack, resplendent in uniform. The well-known charm had worked. General McDonnell, hearing that the wedding had had to be postponed, insisted that his ADC caught the next train to London. (He later wrote to Jack, 'you are a lucky man to own that piece of sunshine.')

The following morning, at the King's Chapel of the Savoy, Jack and Doris became man and wife. Their life together, which should have had every prospect of happiness, had begun. After a hurried reception, replacing the cancelled arrangements, they left for a few days together in the small Devon fishing village of Seaton. In later years, my mother said that she knew on her honeymoon that she had made a grave mistake. After the glamour, the looks, the uniform, the charm had been stripped away, little else was left. More importantly, for someone as highly sexed as Doris, Jack had a total hang-up about the physical side of marriage. In the rigid Calvinistic confines of the kirk, sex was something one never discussed and never enjoyed. Its only purpose was procreation and certainly not fun. (A year or two later, after a few days' separation, she met his train at Leeds station. Her suggestion that they should spend the afternoon in bed was greeted with horror – he seemed to think she had the instincts of a tart.)

The wedding of my parents, Jack and Doris McNaughton, at the King's Chapel of the Savoy, 4 April 1918.

My mother Doris, lively and vivacious even at 18 months old.

The war ended, and Jack had to find something to do. His ideal milieu was the army, in which he had served with distinction, and he once more applied for a regular commission in the Gunners (the Royal Artillery), where one of Norman McNaughton's sons, Forbes, had already found a home.[39] He travelled down to 'The Shop', the Royal Artillery headquarters at Woolwich, and sat the entrance exam. Alas, his limited brain cells let him down. My mother always said that an army career would have been his making, and it was a grave disappointment. With no paper qualifications and nothing to offer save charm, his future looked bleak. However, he had a rich father-in-law who proposed to put him into the family iron and steel works, Monkbridge, where he would learn the trade from the shop floor. Although not entirely to Jack's taste, this was better than nothing. His wife had a large private income (her father had given her a lump sum which produced £600 per annum – an enormous amount in those days – as her dress allowance when she married.) He was not to be so generous with his six remaining daughters, as his first son-in-law proceeded to run

My mother Doris (centre, aged four) with her two elder sisters Sylvia (left, eight) and Evelyn (six).

through the money. Wives had little control over their own money, and, in any case, Doris was still so besotted with her husband that she gave him whatever he asked. Most of it went on gambling, drink and greyhounds.[40]

They bought an attractive country house, Longwood, built in the local Yorkshire stone and with a large, spacious garden, near Shadwell, a village a few miles north of Leeds. Here they settled down to raise their family. (When in 1982 I tracked the house

604a Waterhead Windermere

Do you see any likeness to Violet?

An unkind post-
card from my
mother Doris to
her younger sister
Enid, *c* 1912.

down, the setting was no longer rural, but in the vast suburban
purlieus of Moortown. A large housing estate, 'Longwood Close',
has been built on the site of the long-demolished house.)

On 10 June 1920, Doris gave birth to her first son, Alexander,
or Aleck as he was usually called. All seemed well at first and the
baby flourished. But one day, when he was six months old, my
mother went to his pram to find him dead. Her grief can only be
imagined. There was no knowledge of a 'cot death' syndrome in
those days and his death seemed inexplicable. Two years later, on
10 February 1922, another son was born, Anthony. Three months
before his birth, my mother had been carrying a heavy vase of flowers and slipped on the polished floor. Trying not to break the vase,
she fell heavily. It was not until the birth of the baby that doctors
discovered his spine had been damaged – he was in fact a spina bi-
fida baby. At six weeks old, it was decided to operate. He did not
survive. The loss of two sons in such a short space of time must
have been agonising. Her parents had little tact or sensitivity. 'You
and Jack don't seem very good at having babies,' said her father
afterwards, 'you'd better not have any more.'[41]

108

Evelyn (Beve), my mother's favourite sister, aged about 18.

Doris McNaughton at the time of her marriage, aged about 23.

After this double tragedy, my parents drifted apart. Jack spent more time with his golfing and drinking cronies and Doris sought sexual release elsewhere. Among her many lovers was the purser of the cruise ship in which they travelled to the Canaries for a holiday.[42]

Despite her father's unkind warning, my mother was determined to have another child. In February 1925 she and Jack went on a skiing holiday to Lenzerheide, in Switzerland. It was here, among the Alpine peaks, that I was supposedly conceived, and on 18 November 1925 I was born in my mother's bedroom at Longwood, Moortown, Leeds. My mother, a strong-minded woman, did not want an only child and on 24 July 1927 my sister, Margaret Evelyn, was born.[43] My mother told me later that it had taken all her wiles to get Jack into bed.

My mother Doris with her second son Anthony, born 10 February 1922, died 24 March 1922.

Meanwhile, four of the sisters had married. Evelyn had fallen in love with a handsome Australian barrister, Oscar Nevett, who had come to England to enlist and had won the M.C. In 1919 she married him and they sailed for Melbourne, where he had a thriving legal practice. This was a devastating blow for my mother, for Evelyn was her best friend, and she now saw her only on their rare visits home. They had five children: Jane, Doris, Chester, Anne and Guy. Three of the remaining sisters found complacent husbands, all delighted to be gathered into the Kitson fold. The following year, Marguerite Emily (or Sylvia, as she preferred to be called) married the Reverend Halstead Connor, the brother of their former governess, 'Emmy' Wharton. A dull clergyman, he later had the living of Benhall, near Saxmundham, Suffolk, and I remember having to sit through his tedious sermons. Sadly, they had no children. Two years later, Violet found her lifelong mate. Her bridegroom was William Shiell, who came from Scotland. He seemed to have plenty of money – so much, in fact, that he never appeared to do anything; his brother, Alec, moved in homosexual circles and

The marriage of Evelyn Kitson and Oscar Nevett M.C., 1919; Evelyn's sisters Violet and Angela acted as bridesmaids.

The marriage of Sylvia (or Marguerite Emily) Kitson and the Reverend Halstead Connor, 1920. The bride's mother appears to have worn the same rather striking hat for both ceremonies, though on this occasion the ears pointed upwards.

The marriage of Violet Kitson and William Shiell, 1922; Violet's younger sister Thelma is the bridesmaid on the left.

The marriage of Thelma Kitson and Dr Noel Harris, 1923; Angela, the youngest of the seven Kitson sisters and the last to marry, is standing at the far right.

The marriage of Enid Kitson and Stewart McNaughton, 1924, at St Columba's Pont Street, Knightsbridge.

THE MARRIAGE OF LORD AIREDALE'S FOURTH DAUGHTER: THE HON. ENID KITSON AND MR. STEWART McNAUGHTON LEAVING ST. COLUMBA'S.

was a close friend of Terence Rattigan and Denholm Elliott. Uncle Will collected pictures, some of them rather good. One day, my mother arrived at their house to be greeted by Violet with the words 'Oh, you must come and see my new Raeburn.' Thinking that she was going into the kitchen to admire a new cooker, she was surprised to find a ravishing portrait by Sir Henry Raeburn, above the drawing-room chimneypiece. They lived in some style in a large and imposing house, Chalden House, Hemel Hempstead, and produced four children, a boy and three girls. John, whom I re-member as a shy, bespectacled youth, was born in 1922. After sur-viving only one year at Eton, he joined the Royal Tank Corps, and died of leukaemia in 1942. Next came Cynthia, an attractive red-head.[44] The second daughter, Mary, a clever girl who read Greats at Oxford, married Charles Montague, a widowed schoolmaster, with whom she opened a finishing school for foreign students near Sevenoaks. She is now widowed and lives near Halesworth. The third sister is Janet, who married Julian Morgan.

A year later, Thelma married Noel Harris.[45] Good-looking, charming and with a keen sense of humour, Noel became a psychiatrist, and they lived on site at Springfield Mental Hospital, Tooting. (Years later, Thelma infuriated me, referring to my beloved Catherine, when she said 'Oh, I've had a lot of experience with the mentally deficient.' The Kitsons, or rather the Schuncks, were incredibly insensitive.) The marriage was not happy, and early in his career Noel had an affair with one of his daughters' governesses. Despite this, he and Thelma produced three girls. Joyce married Edward Griffith, a colleague of her father; Beryl married Michael Johnson; and Jean chose Jimmy Arnot. Noel and Thelma

The marriage of Angela Kitson and George Goff, 1927.

The Harris family in about 1934.

longed for a son, but he did not appear. Beryl told me, years later, that as a last resort her parents had tried making love upside down. This had the desired result in Gordon, who became a solicitor. (In his teens he decided to call himself 'Jim'.) He later married Primrose Mallet,[46] of Mallet Court, Curry Mallet, Somerset.[47]

Five down and two to go. By 1924 there were still two sisters unspoken for. Angela, the youngest, who was 19, and Enid, now 26 and on the shelf. Where could she find a husband? Was it her parents, or Jack and his father, or perhaps my mother, who thought of the still unattached Stewart? Jack's younger brother had survived the war and become a chartered accountant. Despite his lack of looks, he was intelligent, studious, reliable with a dry wit, in every way unlike his sibling. Stewart needed no encouragement: he would emulate his much-loved elder brother and join the Kitson clan. They were married by the bridegroom's father at St Columba's, the Scottish church in Pont Street, Knightsbridge, on 26 April 1924. The bride was attended by four bridesmaids, her sister Angela, Christine Kitson (a cousin), Shirley Preston and Peggy Wolfe-Barry. They wore 'apricot charmeuse dresses with the skirts made of two deep accordion pleated flounces worn with

Enid Kitson aged about 18.

The children of Enid and Stewart McNaughton c 1933: Alison, aged four; Margaret, six; and Ronald, eight.

silver-leaf bandeaux finished with flowing streamers of apricot tulle'. The bride's dress was of ivory charmeuse with a diamante girdle. On her head she wore a diamante coronet which held in place a fine old veil of Honiton lace, lent by the Hon. Hilda Kitson. The best man was Hew Hedderwick. Among the distinguished guests were Lord and Lady Southwark, Lady Roxburgh and Lady Kensington.[48]

After a short spell in London, the couple moved to Stansted, Essex, where their house, Roycot, proved a haven of comfort to their many relations. Although Enid was not intelligent and had little humour,[49] she was a kindly woman who proved to be a good cook, despite never having been taught. (Sadly, like those of most of her sisters, her marriage was not happy. For several years, Stewart's girlfriend in Stansted was Eleanor, the wife of Basil Irwin, my husband's boss at the Ionian).

Stewart and Enid produced three good-looking children. Like his uncle Jack, Ronald, the eldest, could never win paternal approval. He followed his father to Cargilfield and Fettes, enlisted in the Royal Navy as an Ordinary Seaman, and made two unfortunate marriages. The first, to Patricia Webster, a riding school instructress, produced a daughter, Fiona. In 1963 they moved to Grantown-on-Spey where Ronald managed the Craiglynne Hotel. His wife ran a successful riding school and won several prizes for her ponies. But Patricia was not happy and suffered from the painful skin disease psoriasis. After Stewart's death from prostate cancer in 1972, Enid sold Roycot and moved to Scotland to be with her son.[50] With the proceeds of the sale, she bought Ronald his own hotel at Holm Hill and built a bungalow for the family in the grounds. It was here, on the evening of 8 December 1976, after a long day in the hotel, that Ronald returned home to find the body of his wife swinging from a beam.[51]

After this traumatic event, Ronald escaped on a cruise, where he was picked up by a widow, Margaret Robb, a music teacher. Mrs Robb's husband, a high flyer in an oil company, had been killed in an air crash and his widow had received a large pay-out. Five months after his wife's suicide, Ronald married her. (I met her when I was in Edinburgh in 1979. She was big, blowsy and bottle-blond, and I did not take to her. She told me at length of the money

Ronald McNaughton (seated second from the right), a distraught widower, in February 1977.

she had and paraded in her 'cruise wear'.) The marriage did not last, and in 1981 they were divorced. She was a clever woman and as part of the divorce settlement acquired most of the fine McNaughton furniture and pictures that Ronald had inherited. Three years later, he died in an Edinburgh nursing home of prostate cancer, aged 59.

Ronald's daughter, Fiona, having made an unhappy marriage to Paul Scott, a landscape gardener, had a daughter, Rachel. After her parents' divorce, Rachel and her mother became estranged and she was brought up by her father's parents.[52] Latterly, Fiona met a man called Alan, who adored her. They had a short time of happiness together before Fiona died of breast cancer, aged 44. After Ronald, Stewart and Enid had two daughters, Margaret, who would become a beauty, and Alison, almost as pretty, with the determined McNaughton chin. The dreaded cancer gene would claim them both – Alison in 1967, aged 36, and Margaret in 1969, aged 42.

In 1927, the last of the seven Kitson sisters married. Angela, aged 22 and a lively girl, chose the 40-year-old George Goff, bluff, genial and heavily built; he was something to do with Indian railways. They made their home in Dacca. George had a maiden sister, Beatrix, who owned a series of fat Pekineses. George and Angela produced two children, Stephen, born in 1928, and Jennifer, two years younger.

And so, thanks to the largesse of the Kitson family, all seven found husbands.

* * *

On 8 June 1925, my paternal grandfather retired from his living in Galloway, aged 70, and was presented by his parishioners with a beautiful picture of the hills near Carsphairn painted by George Houston. (A copy hung at Roycot, Stewart's home.) Thereafter 'Dad', as he was always called, made his home with Stewart and Enid, leaving it for brief sorties to his elder son in Leeds. He was a firm favourite with my Airedale grandfather, and they would fish together in Skye. A remarkable and lovely man, he and Doris were devoted to each other. He undertook her neglected education and taught her to love reading.. He gave her a complete set of Dickens

My grandfather the Reverend G. F. A. McNaughton, aged about 60.

as a wedding present. He was a keen and knowledgeable botanist, and owned a fine set of wild flower books, bound in blue leather. I now realise, having researched his family of booksellers and publishers, that my literary traits come from him.

His favourite psalm was number 121:

> I will lift up my eyes unto the hills from whence cometh my help.
> My help cometh from the Lord which made heaven and earth.
> He will not suffer thy foot to be moved: he that keepeth thee will not slumber
> Behold, he that keepeth Israel shall neither slumber nor sleep.
> The Lord is thy keeper: the Lord is thy shade upon thy right hand.
> The sun shall not smite thee by day, nor the moon by night.
> The Lord shall preserve thee from all evil: he shall preserve thy soul.
> The Lord shall preserve thy going out and thy coming in from this time forth,
> and
> Even for evermore.

And his favourite Shakespeare sonnet was number 33:

> Full many a glorious morning have I seen,
> Flatter the mountain tops with sovereign eye,
> Kissing with golden face the meadows green,
> Gilding pale streams with heavenly alchemy,
> Anon permit the basest clouds to ride
> With ugly rack on his celestial face,
> And from the forlorn world his visage hide,
> Stealing unseen to west with this disgrace.
> Even so my sun one early morn did shine
> With all triumphant splendour on my brow;
> But out, alack, he was but one hour mine,
> The region cloud hath masked him from me now.
>   Yet him for this my love no whit disdaineth;
>   Suns of the world may stain when heaven's sun staineth.

This is why I would like *Hills of the North Rejoice* and also Psalm 121 at my funeral because it will remind me of him. He loved the hills of his northern home.

Although I was only seven years old when he died, my memories of him are much sharper than those of either of my two Airedale grandparents, who died when I was almost grown-up. I remember the walks he took us as children down the Yorkshire lanes, pointing out the wild flowers which he loved so well – campion, mallow, herb Robert. He was a man of God and his goodness shone out.

On 11 April 1933, the life of this saintly man came to an end. He died at Roycot, Stansted, with his younger son Stewart at his bedside. He was 78 years old. The cause of death was given as 'My-ocardial Disease – Atheroma of the Aorta and Arterio-Sclerosis'. There was no post-mortem. His remains were borne back to Scotland, to the small Galloway parish of Carsphairn, which had been his home for so long. Here he was mourned by his many friends and parishioners and was laid to rest beside his beloved wife.

Here endeth Volume One.

The rest will follow
si mihi parcitur [53]

Thomas Hemsley,
Lord Airedale's
devoted butler
(see page 102).

Notes

1. Born 4 January 1855. His parents were James McNaughton, born 2 January 1807 at Caputh, Perthshire, and Helen (always known as Ellen) Ferrier (born 2 January 1817), of North Leith, Edinburgh, whose late father, William, was a bookbinder. They were married, at North Leith on 20 March 1851. He was a widower, his first wife having died some years earlier.

2. A family connection was Susan Ferrier, the celebrated 18th-century novelist. See Appendix 1.

3. There is still a Ferrier's bookshop in Edinburgh today.

4. Holidays were spent with their Strain cousins Hilly (later Wyllie) and Nell (Wolfe-Barry) at Cassilis (pronounced Cassels) House, Ayrshire, which John Strain rented from the Marquess of Ailsa, to whom the McNaughtons were connected through the Ferriers.

5. Born 27 September 1853 at Bield Cottage, Linlithgow, Scotland. Died 11 February 1918 at 61 De Parys Avenue, Bedford.

6. Born 26 January 1857. According to my second cousin, John Hawkesworth, David Norman's grandson, he and my grandfather, George, held the go-slow record for going round Prestwick golf course in seven hours!

7. See Chapter 1 for more information on my grandfather's family.

8. Margaret Ferrier Anderson, born 7 April 1862, daughter of John Anderson (born 14 March y.n.k.), a drysalter and ironmonger, and Margaret Finlayson, born 14 March (y.n.k.). I believe Margaret Anderson's sister was Catherine Taylor (born 1 March y.n.k.), who was always known as 'Aunt Kate'; her beautifully monogrammed initials are embroidered on much of our linen. She was my godmother, and I was called by my first name after her. She married William Gray (Uncle Willy), of Gray, Dunn biscuits. My grandmother's brother, also Willy (Uncle Willy Anderson), owned a gold hunter that has passed down to us; turned upside down, his monogram, W.A., becomes W.M.

9. Jack (christened John), born 20 February 1892; George Stewart Burns, born 13 June 1894.

10. A photograph of Jack, aged about four, is on my dressing-table and appears on page 88 of this book.

11. *The Manse Cookery Book* has recipes for both Floating Island and Bessie's girdle scones written in my grandmother's neat hand in a thick exercise book which may be in the attic with other papers.

12. I always kept it in my jewel box, stolen in the Reedham burglary.

13. George V and Edward, Prince of Wales

14. Presumably for entry to either the Royal Military Academy, Sandhurst, or to the Royal Military Academy at Woolwich ('the Shop'), which prepared officers for the Artillery (the 'Gunners') and the Engineers.

15. See Appendix 4 for a detailed account of the raid.

16. Both were 'sons of the Manse' and were referred to by their comrades as 'bloody Ministers' sons'.

17. His many letters from Egypt and Gallipoli have been lent to me by Stewart's grandson, Mark Landale.

18. W.R. Mill to the Reverend G.F.A. McNaughton, 11 September 1915.

19 Comment from his brother, enduring the heat of the Western Desert, in a letter dated 6 April 1916.

20 G.S.B. McNaughton to his cousin, Hilary Strain, 11 September 1915.

21 An iron kettle or pot used by soldiers to make tea or stew.

22 He was quite short – about 5 foot 5 inches.

23 G.S.B. McNaughton to his father, 8 December 1915.

24 The son of Sir John Wilson, 1st baronet, chairman of Wilsons and Clyde Coal Co. Ltd, and MP for Falkirk.

25 The carnage wrought by the Great War was relentless. Tom Wilson was killed in 1917, and his sister Jane's first husband, Colonel Monteith of the Bedfordshires, in 1915. Their son, Jack, was born 2 days before his father's death in 1915 (he later commanded the 2nd Battalion The Black Watch Royal Highland Regiment) and she married, secondly, General Sir Reginald May.

26 That went to his half-brother, Roland, the 3rd Baron, High Sheriff of London in 1928 and Chairman of Fords, 1928.

27 John Edward Darnton, *The Von Schunck Family*, privately published 1933.

28 See the website about him: www.chriscooksey.demon.co.uk/schunck . I have received much help from Chris Cooksey, its compiler.

29 We have a first edition of *Alice in Wonderland* signed 'From Dr. Schunck to Florence Schunck'. I think this must be the eminent uncle Edward rather than Florence's father.

30 *c* 1833–1913. The Lupton in the firm of solicitors Dibb, Lupton & Co., is a descendant of Kate Lupton's family.

31 born *c* 1807; mayor of Leeds 1844.

32 His house near the village of Roundhay, Leeds.

33 According to my cousin Mary Montague, our grandfather had an unfortunate riding accident as a young man. This did not render him impotent, as might be supposed, but had the opposite effect. Thelma (one of my mother's sisters) told her daughter Beryl how their father would chase her round the drawing-room. She was so frightened that she locked her bedroom door. Presumably, by this time, his wife had locked hers too.

34 Christened Marguerite Emily, after her mother's sister, she changed her name to 'Sylvia' when she was about to enter a convent. However, Halstead Connor, brother of her governess, Emily Connor, saved her from this fate when he married her. (Saint Silvia, 515–92, the mother of St Gregory, was renowned for her piety.)

35 He was rather vague about the identity of his family. Once, when walking in Hyde Park with a friend, who saw a group of girls on the horizon, the latter asked him, 'Oh, by the way, Airedale, isn't that your family over there?' My grandfather replied, 'You may be right. I recognise the governess'.

36 See Appendix 4.

37 Sir Walter Scott, 'Oh, Young Lochinvar came out of the West'.

38 Stewart to Jack, 3 August 1916.

39 In the Royal Horse Artillery. Forbes, who possessed the celebrated McNaughton charisma, was one of Norman McNaughton's four sons. An

outrageous flirt, he was irresistible to women, but, unlike my father, was able to deliver. (Two more of Norman's sons, Hamish and Norman George, were killed during the First World War. Norman George, who won the M.C. in the Royal Flying Corps, was shot down by the German air ace, Baron von Richthofen, known as 'the Red Baron', in 1915.) 2nd Lieutenant Hamish McNaughton was killed in France on 23 April 1917, three days before his brother Norman was reported missing in France or Belgium. Such was the carnage of the First World War.

40 My grandfather took care that none of the remaining six daughters had control of their own money. It was tightly tied up in trusts. He had learned his lesson – too late for Doris.

41 In today's climate, the loss of two babies would have alerted social workers, my mother might have been accused of murder, for which the death sentence then applied, and I would probably have been 'taken into care'.

42 I have often wondered about my paternity – my father and I had absolutely nothing in common except our love of books and a tendency to constipation.

43 Always known as 'Peggy', which she disliked.

44 Cynthia joined the Wrens and married Lieutenant Aubone St Vincent Hammick, Royal Navy, a tall 'Dart' nicknamed Spike because of his height.

45 The son of Sir Charles Alexander Harris, Governor of Newfoundland 1917–22.

46 Diana Lang, an old friend, remembers her in the hunting field.

47 Apparently his mother-in-law, a formidable woman, did not approve of the name 'Gordon'. She insisted on calling him 'James'.

48 Report in *The Times*, 28 April 1924. Courtesy of Donald McNaughton.

49 Occasional shafts of humour would appear. I once regaled Enid with a saga of how I had been pole-axed with period pain at Liverpool Street station and the kindly waiting room attendant had rushed off to heat a dinner plate to place on my recumbent tummy. She laughed and laughed till the tears were rolling down her face.

50 Her Scottish sojourn was not long. In 1974 she died in a Grantown hospital from a stroke, aged 75.

51 A photograph of Ronald with fellow Grantown hoteliers, taken two months later, shows a man distraught. It appears on page 119.

52 Rachel is now living happily with her partner, Russell Savage, in Nairn, where she has a successful hairdressing business.

53 'if I am spared.'

Appendix 1

Ferrier, Susan Edmonstone (1782–1854), novelist, was born on 7 September 1782 in Edinburgh, the ninth of the ten surviving children of James Ferrier (1744–1829), writer to the signet, and his wife, Helen (1741–97), daughter of Robert Coutts, a farmer near Montrose. James Ferrier, who came from Linlithgow, had a legal practice in Edinburgh and included John, fifth duke of Argyll among his clients and friends; his appointment as principal clerk of session in 1802 owed much to Argyll's influence. In 1784 Ferrier and his family moved from Lady Stair's Close, where Susan was probably born, to 11 George Street, a house in the Georgian New Town. Susan Ferrier was educated at home, and as her father was well established in Edinburgh's close-knit society, she and his other children came to know many of its notable figures, not least Sir Walter Scott and Henry Mackenzie.

James Ferrier frequently went to Inveraray on Argyll's business, and in 1797 he took Susan on her first visit. Large house parties were often held there and the duke's daughters, Lady Augusta Clavering and Lady Charlotte Campbell (later Lady Charlotte Bury), encouraged private theatricals and the production of a weekly journal. Susan Ferrier became a close friend of the family and in particular of the duke's granddaughter, Charlotte Clavering, with whom she maintained a lively correspondence. By about 1810 they had decided to co-operate in writing a novel, but a major obstacle to this project was the difference in style and ability of the two authors. The novel, eventually published as *Marriage* in 1818, was wholly Susan Ferrier's work except for 'The History of Mrs Douglas', which was contributed by Charlotte Clavering. However, their letters show that Charlotte provided encouragement and criticism throughout, reading passages to Lady Charlotte Campbell and reporting her delighted reaction. William Blackwood, to whom Susan Ferrier sent the unfinished manuscript in 1817, was also enthusiastic, though he offered only £150 for the copyright. The novel was published anonymously and, although a few people guessed the author's identity, Susan Ferrier denied authorship. It was an immediate success, the lively humour and social satire having great appeal. The author had a sharp eye for the foibles of human nature and several of her more eccentric characters such as Lady Maclaughlan and the three aunts at Glenfern Castle were based on real people. Charlotte Clavering had already recognized Lady Maclaughlan's dress as that of the sculptress Anne Seymour Damer, and her manners as those of Lady Frederick Campbell.

After the death of her mother and the marriages of her three elder sisters, Susan Ferrier remained at home to keep house for her father. As was the custom, they would take a house on the outskirts of Edinburgh during the summer months, and it was in East Morningside House that she wrote much of *The Inheritance*, published by Blackwood in 1824. By now, the author's identity was more widely known, but she genuinely wished to remain anonymous. Writing to her sister Helen Kinloch in 1823 she said

> I never will avow myself, and nothing can hurt or offend me so much as any of my friends doing it for me; this is not *façon de parler*, but my real and unalterable feeling. I could not bear the *fuss* of authorism! (Ferrier, Memoir, 178)

The Inheritance was enthusiastically received; Scott, Henry Mackenzie and his daughters, Francis Jeffrey, Basil Hall, and the Argyll family all expressed their delight. Her friends were able to recognize James Ferrier in the character of Uncle Adam Ramsay, and others who read the novel enjoyed speculating on the identity of the characters. '*Everybody* knows who the characters are, but no two people can agree about them. I have heard of five or six Lord Rossvilles and as many Miss Pratts' (Ferrier, *Memoir*, 180). Appreciation of the work was not confined to Scotland; an American edition and a French translation both appeared in 1824 and a Swedish translation in 1836.

The publication of Susan Ferrier's third novel, *Destiny*, in 1831 owed much to her friendship with Scott. She had visited him at Ashestiel in 1811 and again at Abbotsford in 1829 and 1831. They evidently enjoyed each other's company: she thought him delightful, and he wrote of her 'This gifted personage besides having great talents has conversation the least exigeant of any author, female at least ..., simple, full of humour, and exceedingly ready at repartee, and all this without the least affectation of the blue stocking' (*Journal*, 654). Lockhart recorded her tact in helping the ageing Scott over his lapses of memory. Her account of these visits was published posthumously in volume 40 of *Temple Bar* (1874). She dedicated *Destiny* to Scott and it was he who advised her to break with Blackwood and who helped her brother to negotiate publication by Robert Cadell at the greatly enhanced fee of £1700. Thirteen years had passed since the appearance of *Marriage*, and while *Destiny* retains the element of caricature in the figure of the minister Mr M'Dow, its tone is more didactic than that of the earlier novels. Social satire and the mockery of vulgarity have given way to a moralizing approach, reflecting the author's maturer interests. Although it did not prove as popular as *Marriage*, *Destiny* was well received and appealed to readers as diverse as Joanna Baillie and the lord advocate, Andrew Rutherfurd. All three novels are rather weakly plotted, their success lying mainly in the author's keen eye for the ridiculous and her entertaining portrait of Scottish society. Her letters reveal her own tastes in literature: she admired Jane Austen and Scott (though she had reservations about some of his works), but condemned Galt and Lockhart. In 1836, Robert Thorburn painted a miniature, intended to show her as she was about 1812; this was one of his early commissions and he kept in touch with her even after he had established himself successfully in London.

In 1841 Susan Ferrier sold the copyrights on her novels to Richard Bentley, who brought out new, illustrated editions. To her annoyance, *Marriage* did not include her revisions, and she disliked the illustrations. Eleven years later she gave him permission to publish a new edition, the first under her name, on condition that her revisions were incorporated and some of the illustrations removed. Bentley also tried to persuade her to write another novel, but in vain. She had already made several unsuccessful attempts at the request of a friend in 1837. The surviving chapters of a work entitled 'Maplehurst Manor' probably date from that period. Her eyes had been troubling her for some time and towards the end of her life she spent much of her time in a darkened room, but still managed to keep up some cheerful correspondence with her family and friends. Her life had always been quiet; her devoted care for her father and her own poor health discouraged her from travel, though she made occasional visits to friends and relatives in Scotland, and a few to London. Otherwise, she spent her life in Edinburgh, becoming more secluded as her health deteriorated, but maintaining an interest in literature and the church. Like most of her family, she had been a member of the Church of Scotland, but she joined the Free Church after the Disruption of 1843. She died in her brother's house at 38 Albany Street, Edinburgh, on 5 November 1854, and was buried in the family grave in St Cuthbert's churchyard.

ELSPETH YEO

Sources

Memoir and correspondence of Susan Ferrier, 1782–1854, ed. J. A. Doyle (1898) · M. Cullinan, Susan Ferrier (1984) · Susan Ferrier 1782–1854 (1982) [with edn of 'Maplehurst Manor'; exhibition catalogue, NL Scot.] · S. E. Ferrier, 'Recollections of visits to Ashistiel and Abbotsford', Temple Bar, 40 (1874), 329–35 · The journal of Sir Walter Scott, ed. W. E. K. Anderson (1972), 654 · F. R. Hart, The Scottish novel: a critical survey (1978), 57–68 · [J. Ferrier], 'Miss Ferrier's novels', Temple Bar, 54 (1878), 308–28 · Register of the Society of Writers to Her Majesty's Signet (1983), 105 · J. Smith, Monumental inscriptions in St Cuthbert's churchyard, Scottish RS, no. 75 (1915) · parish register, St Cuthbert's

Archives

NL Scot., corresp. and papers

Likenesses

A. Edouart, cut-paper silhouette, c.1831 (of Ferrier or her cousin Margaret?), Scot. NPG · R. Thorburn, miniature, 1836, priv. coll. [see illus.] · J. Gall, marble bust, 1854, priv. coll.; repro. in S. Ferrier, The inheritance (1894), frontispiece

Wealth at death

£777 19s. 4d.: inventory, Edinburgh Commissary Court Records, NA Scot., SC 70/1/85, pp. 148–52

Reproduced from Oxford Dictionary of National Biography by permission of the Delegates of Oxford University Press. Copyright (c) Oxford University Press. All rights reserved.
For further information, see the ODNB's website at www.oxforddnb.com.

Appendix 2

Kitson, James (1807–1885), ironmaster and locomotive builder, was born in Leeds on 27 October 1807, the eldest of six children of a licensed victualler and his wife. He may be the James Kitson who was baptized in Leeds on 3 January 1808, the son of William Kitson. He was educated at local schools and at the Leeds Mechanics' Institution and Literary Society, where he was a diligent student in drawing and mathematics. On 20 September 1828 he married Ann, daughter of John Newton, owner of a painting and decorating firm. They had four sons and two daughters.

Encouraged by his studies of *A Practical Treatise on Rail-Roads*, by Nicholas Wood, Kitson quickly realized the great potential future of steam locomotive traction and in 1837 he joined Charles Todd, who had been apprenticed to James Fenton of the locomotive builders Fenton, Murray, and Jackson, and David Laird, a farmer and financier, in establishing Todd, Kitson, and Laird at the Railway foundry in Leeds, manufacturers of machinery and locomotives.

In 1838 six locomotives were built for the Liverpool and Manchester Railway. In 1839 Kitson and Laird withdrew from this partnership and established the Airedale foundry, also in Leeds, whose first locomotives were built for the North Midland Railway in 1840. David Laird withdrew in 1842 and the firm was reconstituted as Kitson, Thompson, and Hewitson. Large numbers of locomotives were built for home and overseas railways. Among these was the 0–6–0 type (1849) with inside cylinders and frames, for the Leeds and Thirsk Railway, a design which established the standard for freight locomotives in Britain over many decades. The first export locomotives (for the Orléans–Bordeaux railway) were built in 1846, followed by those for the Kiel–Altona line in 1848, and many more for India, Australia, South Africa, South America, and elsewhere.

Kitson's great organizing ability, technical ingenuity, and grasp of industrial developments formed the mainspring of these activities. In 1854 he felt it desirable to acquire a source of good

Yorkshire iron for the Airedale foundry and established the Monk Bridge ironworks nearby, which was managed by his sons Frederick William and James Kitson (later first Baron Airedale), the former having previously been principal locomotive designer at Airedale. After the retirement of Isaac Thompson in 1858 and the death of William Hewitson in 1863 the Kitson family took complete control of the firm, and later James Kitson, junior, and the third son, John Hawthorn, who managed the Airedale foundry from 1863, became partners with their father.

Kitson's first wife died and on 24 January 1868 he married Elizabeth, daughter of the Revd John E. Scroope Hutchinson, vicar of East Stoke, Nottinghamshire. They had two sons and two daughters. Kitson retired from the business in 1876, but was a man of wide interests and many activities outside his industrial work. Very musical and with a fine voice, in his youth he had built an organ in an outhouse of his father's premises. Later he became chairman of the orchestral committee for the Leeds music festival. He was also chairman of the Leeds Northern Railway and later a director of the North Eastern Railway. He was vice-chairman and later chairman of the Yorkshire Banking Company. An alderman of Leeds in 1858–68, he was mayor in 1860–61, as well as being a magistrate for Leeds borough and for the West Riding of Yorkshire. Kitson died at Elmet Hall, Roundhay, Leeds, on 30 June 1885.

GEORGE W. CARPENTER, rev.

Sources
Engineering (3 July 1885) · E. Kitson Clark, *Kitsons of Leeds, 1837–1937* (1938) · E. L. Ahrons, *The British steam railway locomotive, 1825–1925* (1927) · *CGPLA Eng. & Wales* (1885)

Likenesses
bust, Institution of Mechanical Engineers, London

Wealth at death
£100: probate, 1885

Reproduced from *Oxford Dictionary of National Biography* by permission of the Delegates of Oxford University Press. Copyright (c) Oxford University Press. All rights reserved.
For further information, see the ODNB's website at www.oxforddnb.com

Appendix 3

Kitson, James, first Baron Airedale (1835–1911), locomotive manufacturer and politician, was born on 22 September 1835 at Leeds, the second of four sons of James Kitson (1807–1885) of Elmet Hall, Leeds, and his wife, Ann, daughter of John Newton of Leeds. The elder James Kitson, a man of modest origins, went into partnership as a locomotive manufacturer at the Airedale foundry, Hunslet, at about the time of his second son's birth. This business flourished, so that the younger James was able to attend the Wakefield proprietary school and University College, London, where he studied chemistry and natural sciences.

In 1854, at the age of nineteen, Kitson and his elder brother, Frederick William (1829–1877), were put in charge of a recently established ironworks at Monk Bridge, Leeds, which their father had bought for them. They built Monkbridge into a vast concern. In 1858 it was amalgamated with Airedale foundry, and the business became a limited liability company with a £250,000 capital in 1886, though still exclusively under family control. Frederick withdrew through ill health several years before his death in 1877, and James Kitson was effectively head of the firm from 1862, though his father did not retire until 1876. Kitson married Emily Christiana, daughter of Joseph Cliff of Wortley, Leeds, on 20 June 1860. They had three sons and two daughters. After her death in 1873, he married Mary Laura, daughter of Edward Fisher Smith, of Dudley, on 1 June 1881, with whom he had a son and a daughter. Kitson was assisted in running the firm by his younger brother John Hawthorn Kitson (1843–1899), and later by sons and nephews.

The Airedale foundry principally made railway locomotives, producing, from the time of its inception until the end of the nineteenth century, almost 6000 engines for the home market and for export to twenty-eight other countries. There was also diversification into stationary engines for agricultural machinery, and steam engines for tramways. From the 1880s, the Monkbridge works made steel on the Siemens–Martin open-hearth process. Airedale and Monkbridge each employed about 2000 workers at the time of Kitson's death in 1911. Kitson was prominent in business circles: he was president of the Leeds chamber of commerce (1880–81), president of the Iron and Steel Institute (1889–91), and recipient of its Bessemer gold medal in 1903; he served as a member of the council of the Institution of Civil Engineers (1899–1901), and was a member of the Institution of Mechanical Engineers from 1859; he was also president of the Iron Trade Association. Other business interests included chairmanships of the Yorkshire Banking Company, the London and Northern Steamship Company, and the Baku Russian Petroleum Company, and directorships of the London City and Midland Bank and the North Eastern Railway Company.

Kitson had been a member of the Mill Hill Unitarian Chapel since childhood, from the time his family left the Church of England. He was devoted to the Unitarians for the rest of his life; he taught in Sunday school, and served as superintendent and later as chairman of the chapel's trustees. A memorial window to him was unveiled there in 1916. His interests included social and educational work, and at an early age he became prominent in the mechanics' institute movement, helping to establish a branch in Holbeck, and acting as secretary of the Yorkshire Union of Mechanics' Institutes for seven years. Kitson was involved in launching a self-help model dwelling scheme in 1862, designed to enable working men to buy houses on easy terms, though run as a business rather than a charity. He was also a governor of the Leeds General Infirmary and contributed to organizations involved in treating tuberculosis and in training nurses. He supported the Yorkshire College, later the University of Leeds, from its inception in the 1870s. He was a member of the Leeds rifle volunteer corps shortly after its foundation in 1859, rising from the ranks to become a captain, and remained honorary colonel until 1905.

It was Kitson's long-standing interest in education which brought an introduction to national politics during the controversy following the passage of W. E. Forster's Education Act in 1870. He was instrumental in forming a branch of the National Education League in Leeds, becoming secretary and a member of its national council. In 1880 he was president of the Leeds Liberal Association, running the campaign for W. E. Gladstone's election as member of parliament, with great success. Gladstone was also elected for Midlothian, and at a by-election the Leeds seat passed to his son, Herbert. Kitson retained a cordial relationship with Gladstone, and organized his notable visit to Leeds in October 1881, during which the prime minister stayed at Kitson's house, Spring Bank in Headingley. Kitson supported Gladstone over Irish home rule. As president of the National Liberal Federation from 1883 until 1890, he kept it out of the hands of the Liberal Unionists. Standing as a Gladstonian Liberal, Kitson became member of parliament for the Colne Valley in 1892, holding the seat until 1907. During his parliamentary career he was a prominent campaigner for old-age pensions. He also served as the first lord mayor of Leeds, in 1896–7, although never a member of the council. He was created a baronet in 1886, was sworn of the privy council in 1906, and became Baron Airedale of Gledhow in 1907. Other honours included an honorary degree of DSc from the University of Leeds in 1904, and the freedom of his home city in 1906.

Airedale died at the Hotel Meurice in Paris on 16 March 1911, after suffering a heart attack while returning by train from the south of France. After a funeral service at Mill Hill, his body was taken on 22 March to Roundhay church for burial, along a route lined by 4000 workpeople. A memorial service attended by a hundred MPs was held at St Margaret's Church, Westminster.

GILLIAN COOKSON

Sources
Leeds Mercury (17 March 1911) · Yorkshire Post (17 March 1911) · Yorkshire Observer (17 March 1911) · The Times (17 March 1911) · The Guardian (17 March 1911) · Institution of Mechanical Engineers: Proceedings (1911), 409 · W. G. Rimmer, 'Kitson, James', DBB · GEC, Peerage · W. H. Scott, The West Riding of Yorkshire at the opening of the twentieth century: contemporary biographies, ed. W. T. Pike (1902), 109 · C. Hargrove, In memory of James Kitson, 1st Baron Airedale (1911) · Institution of Mechanical Engineers: Proceedings (1878), 11 [obit. of Frederick William Kitson] · Institution of Mechanical Engineers: Proceedings (1899), 269 [obit. of John Hawthorn Kitson] · E. K. Clark, Kitsons of Leeds, 1837–1937 (1938) Gladstone, Diaries

Archives

W. Yorks. AS, Leeds, letters and photographs | BL, corresp. with Lord Gladstone, Add. MSS 46027–46028 · BL, corresp. with W. E. Gladstone, Add. MSS 44472–44789 *passim*, 46044, fols. 8–23

Likenesses

J. S. Sargent, portrait, 1905; in possession of the family, Gledhow Hall, Leeds, 1912 · Spruce, bust, 1911; formerly, Leeds town hall · B. Stone, photograph, NPG · photograph, repro. in Rimmer, 'Kitson, James' · photograph, repro. in Pike, ed., *The West Riding of Yorkshire* · photograph, repro. in Yorkshire Observer · photograph, repro. in Hargrove, *In memory of James Kitson*

Wealth at death

£1,000,000: probate, 31 March 1911, *CGPLA Eng. & Wales*

Reproduced from *Oxford Dictionary of National Biography* by permission of the Delegates of Oxford University Press. Copyright (c) Oxford University Press. All rights reserved.
For further information, see the ODNB's website at www.oxforddnb.com

Appendix 4

Extract from *The 42nd Battalion CEF Royal Highlanders of Canada In the Great War* by Lieutenant Colonel C. Beresford Topp DSO, MC

1917

The closing of the old year found the Battalion again in the front line preparing to celebrate the arrival of the new year by carrying out raid against an enemy post near Common Crater. A good deal of information concerning this post had previously been gathered by patrolling and the operation decided upon was carried out by a party of nine comprising Lieutenant John MacNaughton and Lieutenant C.S.Martin, Sergeants Bealer and Smith, Corporal Plowe and Privates Maquard, Sedgwick, Richardson and Hepburn.

The raid was typical of many such sorties carried out by units of the Canadian Corps and in which the Corps became highly proficient. They not only resulted in a sure means of identification of enemy formations, but seriously undermined his morale, while at the same time building up a spirit of confidence among the raiding troops which was invaluable in the attack on Vimy Ridge. The unadorned official report of this particular one follows:

'Lieutenant MacNaughton went out in advance and placed a covering party of bombers about five yards in front of the German wire in the centre of the gap between Common and Birkin Craters. Lieutenant Martin followed with Sergeant Bealer, Sergeant Smith and Private Maquard and on reaching the covering party they were joined by Lieutenant MacNaughton. The party then proceeded round the lip of Common Crater. They worked their way through the enemy wire and entered his trench. They proceeded along the trench for a short distance and on account of the mud being so heavy it was decided to split the party, and move along the parapet and parados. Lieutenant MacNaughton and Sergeant Bealer followed the parados and Lieutenant Martin, Sergeant Smith and Private Maquard the parapet, until they got to a point near a junction with a communication trench immediately to the right of Birkin

Crater where an enemy post was suspected. After waiting at this junction for about twenty minutes, two enemy sentries were observed, one in an improvised shelter, the other in the trench, the latter a moving patrol. As the sentry approached the raiding party, Sergeant Bealer slipped into the trench, held him up at the point of a revolver and forced him to surrender. At the same time Private Maquard assuming to be the Sergeant-Major called the second sentry from his shelter. The latter came to the entrance and finding himself surrounded dropped his rifle and threw up his hands. The party then proceeded back and reached our trenches with two prisoners at 3.05 a.m. without casualties. Both prisoners belonged to the 23r[d] R.I.R.'

The brief official report contains small hint of the courage and determination of the members of this little party as with faces blackened against the glare of the Verey lights they cautiously worked their way over the craters through the enemy wire and into his line where, without firing a shot, they captured the garrison of a bombing post and with their prisoners safely withdrew to their own position. Numerous congratulatory messages were received, including one from the Corps Commander as follows: 'The Corps Commander wishes to congratulate the 42nd Battalion on its most successful and enterprising raid.'

Lieutenants MacNaughton and Martin subsequently received the Military Cross for their share in this raid and four of the other ranks were decorated with the Military Medal.

Bibliography

Atholl, 7th Duke of, *Chronicles of the Atholl and Tullibardine Families*, 5 volumes, Ballantyne Press, Edinburgh 1908

Ayr Advertiser, 13 February 1890

Barron, Reverend Douglas, *The Castle of Dunnottar and its History*, Blackwood, Edinburgh 1925

Bartlett, John, *A Complete Concordance to Shakespeare*, Macmillan, London 1990

The Book of Common Prayer

Burt, Steven, *A History of Roundhay Park*, Leeds, 1998

Clark, Edwin Kitson, *Kitsons of Leeds 1837–1937*, Locomotive Publishing Company, London 1938

Cross, F.L., *The Oxford Dictionary of the Christian Church*, Oxford University Press, Oxford 1957

Darnton, John Edward, *The Von Schunck Family*, printed and published privately, 1933

Dickens, Charles, *Bleak House*, Oxford University Press, Oxford, 1910

Dickens, Charles, *Great Expectations*, Oxford University Press, Oxford, 1910

Ferguson, Niall, *The Dundee and Newtyle Railway*, Oakwood Press, Oxford, 1995

Guidebook to Dunnottar Castle, 2001

Griffith, Grosvenor Talbot, *James Kitson and Some Others*, unpublished memoir

Lasdun, Susan, *The Victorians at Home*, Weidenfeld & Nicolson, London, 1981

C.S. Nicholls (ed.), *Dictionary of National Biography. Missing Persons*, Oxford University Press, Oxford, 1993

Phelps, Daphne, *A House in Sicily*, Virago, London, 1999

Wells, Stanley (ed.) *William Shakespeare, the Complete Works*, Clarendon Press, Oxford, 1986

The Times, 30 January 1908

The Times, 28 April 1924

Topp, C. Beresford, *The 42nd Battalion C.E.F. Royal Highlanders of Canada in the Great War*, Gazette Printing Co. Ltd, Montreal, 1931

Wood, Nicholas, *A Practical Treatise on Railroads*, Longman Green, London, 1838

Woodrow, Reverend Robert, *History of the Sufferings of the Church of Scotland*, Edinburgh, 1721

The three eldest Kitson daughters, (l–r) Doris (my mother), Sylvia and Evelyn, painted *c* 1912 by G. Hall Neale (see pp.94, 103, 105, 109).

Index